ultimate
relaxation

eddie and debbie shapiro

a seven step programme for stress-free living

ultimate relaxation

eddie and debbie shapiro

Quadrille

publishing director: **anne furniss**
art director: **mary evans**
editor: **pauline savage**
designers: **simon balley and joanna hill**
special photography: **vic paris**
illustrations: **clive goodyer**
picture research: **nadine bazar**
stylist: **nicki walkinshaw**
production: **vincent smith and candida jackson**

*The authors and publishers would like to stress that this book
expresses the well-informed opinions and experience of the authors.
Although we are confident that almost everyone will benefit from
this book, we can in no way guarantee results of any kind.*

First published in 1999 by
Quadrille Publishing Ltd
Alhambra House
27–31 Charing Cross Road
London WC2H 0LS

Cataloguing in Publication Data: a catalogue record for this
book is available from the British Library.

ISBN 1 899988 92 0

Printed in Hong Kong by Dai Nippon

introduction

For a moment, imagine you are a caveman out with fellow tribe members on a hunt for food. A large bear has been spotted and in response the adrenalin hormone is beginning to pump through your body in anticipation of the forthcoming chase. As you close in on the animal, your heart rate begins to increase, your breathing gets shorter, your stomach muscles tighten and your concentration deepens. The level of adrenalin in your system is rising rapidly as you near the point of attack. The next few moments will determine whether you fight to the kill or have to run for your life.

Now move to the present day, and think of a scenario in your own life when everything seems too much for you to cope with. Perhaps your child has kept you awake all night, but instead of being able to take it easy in the morning you have to be at a business meeting first thing. You get delayed in congested traffic so that you are late, the meeting goes on longer than planned and you have to skip lunch in order to write a report. Then, just as an angry client storms into your office demanding better service, your mother telephones in need of help with her car. In the midst of all this you may not have noticed how your heart rate has increased, your breathing has become shorter, your stomach muscles have tightened and your anxiety level has risen. Adrenalin is pumping through your body in response to the circumstances, but in this case there is no-one to fight and nowhere to run to.

We tend to react to increasing pressure by becoming more and more wound up until we are fraught with tension and physically distressed. Yet it *is* possible to experience the above scenario without getting tense. The key is to find a place of inner calm where we can deal with each issue separately as it arises. The tools that we can use to get to that place are relaxation, breathing, meditation and physical movement. They are like a raft that takes us from one side of the river to another, from a state of distress to a state of sanity and emotional balance. They are safe, well-tried and tested techniques – and they work.

This book will lead you through these practices in a Seven Step Programme, so that they become an integral, natural part of your daily life. The techniques are simple and each one of us is capable of practising them and experiencing the benefits. In order to get the most out of the programme, all you will need is a good sense of humour (so that you don't take yourselves too seriously when it all seems too much – laughter is an instant stress-releaser!), a little time (at least half an hour a day) to devote to the exercises, and plenty of patience. In return, you will find that place inside yourself that is always at peace, for it is there inside every one of us.

You will be encouraged to explore all the many facets of your life: your relationship to yourself and to others; your sense of security, confidence and self-esteem; feelings about your work, environment and lifestyle; issues of power, love and forgiveness; and how to bring your innate understanding and insight into everyday living. The more you come to understand yourself, the more you will be willing and able to take an honest look at what you think about yourself and how that self-image may be affecting your health; the way you treat other people and conduct your relationships; how your immediate environment reflects your state of mind; and the ways in which you can make friends with both yourself and your world.

You will also be asked to focus on your priorities – determining what is really important to you and why – and to discover the impulses behind your actions. As you do this you will find a deeper purpose that goes beyond merely fulfilling your needs: you will arrive at a more profound meaning to your entire life.

By following the Seven Step Programme you will learn how to train your mind so that it does not react so quickly and negatively to the pressures of life. The programme comprises physical exercises, relaxation and meditation. You will also find *Time Out* exercises supporting the theme of each part of the book; they are for you to do at any time during the programme to help you focus your mind and overcome any obstacles. The time you spend doing the programme is of value both to you and to all those around you. Your inner peace is the greatest gift you can give to others. When you find a state of inner joy and freedom, there is one less person suffering – you.

the ground of awakening

the stress response

Each one of us has our own relationship to stress, dependent on our life circumstances – what one person finds debilitating or overwhelming may be experienced by another as challenging or exciting. By paying attention to our physical, mental and emotional responses to various situations, we can determine when we are becoming physically compromised by stress, and at what point we have gone beyond our stress-tolerance level. With this self-understanding we can learn how to change a stressful response into a stress-free one.

Cavemen out on a hunt or soldiers on the front line need the stress response in order to have the mental alertness and physical energy to fight; the anticipation of a life-or-death situation puts their entire physiologies into a necessary state of red alert. Harnessed positively, the stress response can enable us to meet challenges and push us into new areas of experience or understanding by heightening our awareness and focusing our attention.

However, the stress most of us are dealing with is not caused by short-lived, life-threatening situations like hunting a bear or waging battle, but is the *distress* that arises from a series of small but mounting pressures. Each incident may appear benign when viewed in isolation, but the accumulation of incidents or demands on us can lead us to feel pressurized. If our response to such pressure is negative, we become increasingly distraught until we are no longer able to maintain our equilibrium. The body will translate this as a crisis and put out the red alert.

The stress response is activated when we are unable adequately to adjust our behaviour or deal creatively with demanding circumstances; our response becomes fearful, we feel overwhelmed and out of control, like a steam cooker coming to full pressure. We are the only ones who can turn down the heat, but we usually feel powerless to do so.

the effects of stress We shall look at the causes of stress in a moment, but first let us explore how stress affects the mind and the body.

The body's response to stress goes through three distinct stages, which Dr Hans Selye has described as the General Adaptation Syndrome (Selye, *The Stress of Life,* New York, McGraw-Hill, 1956). The first stage is the alarm reaction. In the face of what is perceived as a threat or beyond our capability, an immediate physiological reaction prepares the body to respond. This begins in the hypothalamus, a small part of the brain's limbic system that deals with emotions and feelings; this area also monitors the nervous system, the digestion, heart rate, blood pressure and respiration. A red alert causes the release of adrenalin and other hormones which affect these systems. An increased amount of blood is rushed to the brain to help us think more quickly; the heart beats faster, pumping more blood to our muscles, which become tense and ready for action; we start to breathe faster; sugar is released from the liver to give us more energy; digestion slows down; and our hands and feet become clammy as blood shifts away from the skin to be used elsewhere. We are prepared for fight-or-flight.

The second stage is adaptation or resistance. If the stressor is still present after the initial alarm reaction, the body continues to remain in an aroused state,

PHYSICAL SYMPTOMS OF STRESS

★Insomnia and restlessness ★Back and/or shoulder ache, muscle ache ★Skin disorders: rashes, hives, eczema ★Excessive sweating, sweaty hands or feet ★Nervous disorders: twitching, fidgeting, grinding teeth, picking at skin, nail biting ★Immune deficiency illnesses, susceptibility to colds, 'flu, being run down ★Strokes, nerve disorders

★Anxiety, panic ★Irritability, frustration, irrational outbursts of anger, hostility ★Control and power issues ★Depression, feelings of hopelessness/helplessness ★Debilitating fear, insecurity, nervousness

PSYCHOLOGICAL AND EMOTIONAL SYMPTOMS OF STRESS

★Rapid mood changes

★Restlessness ★Impotence, frigidity, loss of sexual interest, promiscuity ★Addictive behaviour, especially concerning cigarettes, alcohol, food or shopping ★Memory loss, impaired concentration, inefficiency, forgetfulness, disorganization ★Paranoia, confusion, self-doubt ★Self-consciousness, lack of self-esteem ★Marital or family problems ★Easily upset or weepy, sadness ★Critical attitudes or judgements, self-criticism ★Numbness of feelings

though this is not as intense as at the first stage. As the crisis starts to recede, the body will start to repair and balance itself, eventually returning to normal.

The third stage is exhaustion. If the stress goes on indefinitely the body is severely compromised. Eventually, it will begin to suffer from what Selye terms 'diseases of adaptation', which include digestive disorders such as heartburn and indigestion, skin conditions such as hives and eczema, high blood pressure, respiratory problems, headaches, and even life-threatening conditions such as heart disease and strokes (see the above chart for further details).

signals and symptoms of stress

As stress has such a wide-ranging effect on us, both physically and emotionally, it is hard to define which illnesses are stress-related and which are not. Conservative estimates suggest that 70 per cent of all illnesses are caused to some degree by stress; others claim that it is more like 90 per cent. Whichever figure is correct, it is evident that stress affects us significantly, so it is essential that we understand it more deeply and learn how to cope with it. In 1997 the British Safety Council estimated that approximately 90 million working days are lost each year due to stress-related problems, at a cost to businesses of about £5 billion, and that more than 150,000 people in Britain now receive counselling as a result of stress; in America, problems caused by stress are reckoned to cost the economy up to $75 billion per year. In a recent US News/Bozell survey, 43 per cent of all adults were described as suffering from noticeable physical and emotional symptoms due to 'burnout'. According to another account, $7,500 per worker each year is lost to stress, through either absenteeism or decreases in productivity while at work.

causes of stress

Few of us like to think of ourselves as people who get stressed. We see being stressed as a sign of weakness, something that happens to life's losers. We prefer to think of stress as something that happens to others, without realizing how susceptible we may be to it ourselves. But, as we have seen, the real cause of stress is not the external circumstances, such as having too many demands and not enough time to fulfil them. The true cause is our perception of the circumstances – whether we see these as fearful, overwhelming, challenging or workable – and our ability to cope with them.

A stressor may be any one of life's big issues – relationship breakdown, moving house, illness or financial pressures – as much as it may be an accumulation of smaller incidents, such as an overcrowded train, spilling a drink, a baby that won't stop crying or too many bills to pay at once. These are life events that we are all subjected to in one way or another, yet for some they will be stress-producing, while for others they will not. The difference lies in our perception of these events.

studies in stress The most comprehensive study of the causes of stress was made by Drs Holmes and Rahe at the University of Washington (Holmes, T. H. & Rahe, R. H., *Journal of Psychosomatic Research II*, 1967). They based their findings on the level of adjustment required for different circumstances, since the inability to adjust adequately to an event is most likely to stimulate the stress response. The Holmes/Rahe Social Readjustment Rating Scale placed the death of a spouse as the most difficult situation to which to adapt, followed by divorce, separation, the death of a close family member, and marriage. In more recent studies, events such as moving house, having a child, financial difficulties, being ill oneself or witnessing the sickness of a close family member, redundancy, a new job, and college examinations have also been rated very highly. To that list we could now add environmental stressors, such as pollution and overcrowding, and a lack of connection with nature.

However, what must be remembered is that we all respond differently to these various life events. A divorce may be high on the list of stressors for one person, but it may come as a welcome relief to another. Our perception of the circumstances, and our belief in how well we can deal with them, are critical. We may have little or no control over the stressors we encounter, but we do have a choice over the way that we view them and the way in which we respond to them.

Many people wrongly believe that it is their work, family or lifestyle that is the sole cause of their stress and that, if they could only stop this or change that, all would be well. However, the stress response arises as a result of our inability to adapt to circumstances. Although changing the life conditions may help, the relief is often only temporary. Invariably, no matter where we go or what we do, we will be easily stressed again, because the changes that need to take place are inside us, not in any external factors.

There is also a popular misconception held by those people who like to live life on a tightrope, such as those involved with sports or in competitive business, that we have to be stressed or 'have an edge' in order to succeed; that the drive of competitiveness or ever greater challenges is needed to stimulate creativity and efficiency, and that without it we would be too inert or passive. In fact, the opposite is true. Stress actually diminishes performance rather than boosting it, and it is only in a truly relaxed state that we can access the kinds of physical and psychological energy required for great creativity.

case history

Helen had a very critical, angry boss, a woman who found fault with everything she was doing, the way she was dressed, and so on. Helen was becoming a nervous wreck. She felt inadequate and shameful, and was developing a real bitterness towards her boss. She wanted to leave, but jobs were scarce in her area. Helen started to practise relaxation and meditation. This gave her a greater objectivity and enabled her to see what an unhappy and sad woman her boss really was underneath her tough exterior. Helen watched her boss moving and talking to other people and saw the loneliness in her body, heard the defeatedness in her voice. Helen then turned her thinking into positive thoughts. Each time her boss approached her she would silently repeat, 'May you be happy, may you be well', while sending her boss thoughts of compassion and love. This lowered her stress response and made her feel calmer and more in control. Soon she was no longer absorbing the criticisms so negatively and was able to talk to her boss more fearlessly until, finally, the criticism stopped. Helen was able to see how her own stress was due to her perception of and reaction to her boss, and in particular to her belief that she herself was at fault. When she saw the reality of this other woman's unhappiness, she saw that all the criticism and anger was due to that sadness, not to anything Helen personally had done.

assessing personal stress levels

This questionnaire will enable you to identify potentially stressful areas in your life and see where you need to bring about change. Find a quiet place where you can sit and have some paper and a pen to hand. Answer the questions that feel most applicable to you and respond as fully and honestly as you can. If you lead a very busy life and have little time to yourself, or if you are supporting and caring for others, you may have high stress levels. The aim is not to create any judgement or blame, but to develop greater self-awareness. As you progress through the book you will find ways to work with your beliefs and understanding of your capabilities, and with those issues that are stressors in your life.

FAMILY

★ Have you recently experienced a death or loss in the family?

★ Have you recently been married, separated or divorced?

★ Has there been a major change in your household, such as a new baby or older children leaving home?

★ Has any member of your family been experiencing a difficult time, such as taking examinations, recovering from an illness, or being in trouble with the police?

★ Is anyone ill and in need of your care?

★ Do you have a healthy relationship with your parents?

★ Do your parents need you or worry you a great deal?

★ Have you been able to share any of these difficulties with anyone?

RELATIONSHIPS

★ Does your partner depend on you or worry you?

★ Do you and your partner disagree about money, the children, your lifestyle?

★ Have you lost your sexual desires?

★ Do you feel bored with your partner?

★ Do you get along with your children?

★ Do you find it difficult to be committed to a relationship?

★ Do you have a friend that you can really talk to?

YOURSELF

★ Do you get time to be alone?

★ Do you get irritated or annoyed easily?

★ Do you dislike your body?

★ Do you care about how you look?

★ Do you worry about the future?

★ Do you always seem to be rushing from one thing to another?

★ Do you cry easily?

★ Do you have an addiction of any sort?

★ Do you feel trapped, or powerless to change anything?

★ Do you panic easily or feel anxious?

★ Is it difficult for you to relax or enjoy yourself in the evenings?

★ Are you able to express your feelings?

★ Do you talk to anyone about your feelings?

★ Do you feel unresolved about past or present concerns?

HEALTH

★ Do you feel tired or get run down easily?

★ Do you do any regular exercise?

★ Do you eat while doing other things, such as working, watching TV, reading the paper, feeding the children?

★ Is television or alcohol your main means of relaxation?

★ Do you eat a lot of snacks, instant or take-away foods?

★ Do you drink more than two cups of coffee a day?

★ Do you spend any part of the day being quiet and reflective?

WORK

★ Do you have to travel to work in crowded trains, buses, or on busy roads?

★ Do you often feel that you have too much to do?

★ Do you often work overtime?

★ Do you feel capable of what is being asked of you?

★ Do you enjoy what you do?

★ Do you take time off for lunch and to rest?

★ Do you dislike your boss?

★ Does your work environment feel depressing? Demoralizing? Loud? Pressured?

★ How do you feel about your colleagues? Intimidated? Angry? Jealous?

★ Do you feel unfulfilled? Unacknowledged? Unrecognized?

★ Would you rather be doing something else?

DREAMS AND ASPIRATIONS

★ If you had more time, how would you like to fill it?

★ If you could have any job in the world, what would it be?

★ If you had the ideal partner, how would it change you?

★ If you felt good about yourself, what would you do differently?

2

the **relaxation** response Most

of us think of relaxation as reading the newspaper in the garden, putting our feet up with a beer and watching a good film, or perhaps going for a drive by the sea. Or we may think we are relaxing when we are engaged in a more physical task, such as walking the dog, painting, or going to a fitness club. Certainly these activities help us to unwind, but too often they deal only with the immediate, more superficial levels of stress. They make us feel better for a while, until the next deadline or traffic jam begins to push us over the edge again.

The relaxation techniques you will learn in this book will give you long-lasting benefits. They will enable you to go deeper, to loosen and release more unconscious levels of stress, those accumulated, unseen tensions that adversely affect our behaviour and health. As we saw in Chapter 1, between 70 and 90 per cent of all illnesses are thought to be caused by stress. This means that a very large proportion of visits to the doctor are for stress-related problems, yet the medical world does not have any adequate remedies for dealing with stress – drugs do not work at changing our workload or life experiences, they simply mask the symptoms.

relaxation and health Relaxation is essential for releasing stress and maintaining good health. If we are in a state of tension – irritable, worried, fearful, pressured or unable to cope – then it is very hard for either the mind or the body to heal itself. The relaxation response affects us physically, mentally and emotionally, easing unconscious layers of tension and reconnecting us with our sanity and peace. The chart opposite shows the differences between various physical and mental states when we are stressed and when we are relaxed.

staying in touch The relaxation response occurs when we learn how to stay in touch with our inner being – with the sanctuary of peace that lies inside each one of us – no matter what is happening around us. We are able to respond to situations without the red flag waving, without adrenalin being

released, without fear, panic or collapse. This means that our physiology remains balanced: the metabolism is not shut down, the heart rate does not increase, our blood pressure stays normal, breathing remains steady and the central nervous system is calmed, thereby slowing excessive nervous activity and relaxing muscles. Energy is not directed towards fight-or-flight, so we have more resources available, increasing our vitality, efficiency and capacity for regeneration.

The health benefits of the relaxation response are enormous. As we release ever deeper levels of stress, so we increase our mental faculties, such as concentration, efficiency, memory and creativity. This gives rise to a state of dynamic relaxation where we are both alert and at ease. A stressed state can hinder our mental performance as too many issues are competing for our attention. In a relaxed state we are able to focus directly and single-mindedly on the task in hand. This

★High blood pressure ★Heart palpitations ★Indigestion, ulcers ★Irritable bowel syndrome, constipation, diarrhoea ★Nervous disorders, muscle tension, backache ★Sexual problems,

STRESSED impotence ★Hyperventilation ★Loss of or excessive appetite ★Excessive sweating ★Insomnia ★Mood swings, irrational behaviour and emotional outbursts ★Problems seem insurmountable, overreaction to making decisions ★Depression, anxiety, addictive behaviour ★Neurosis or phobias ★Excessive anger, resentment, frustration, bitterness, jealousy, fear, panic

♥Blood pressure normalized ♥Regular heartbeat ♥Digestion and metabolism normalized and calmed ♥Intestinal and bowel movement normal ♥Muscle and nerve ease and looseness ♥Sexual

RELAXED confidence ♥Normal and deep breathing ♥Healthy appetite ♥Normal temperature ♥Good sleep ♥Emotional balance ♥Able to stay calm in midst of difficulties ♥Fear and anxiety decrease, addictions overcome ♥Mental balance ♥Development of loving kindness, acceptance, love, peace of mind

generates a greater mental capacity and improved overall performance.

On an emotional level, when we are fully relaxed our feelings of fear, anxiety or hopelessness decrease. This means that we can achieve greater ease within ourselves, be more tolerant and generous with others, and maintain our self-confidence and self-esteem. In a stressed state it is easy to lose touch with compassion and kindness, to focus instead on competitiveness and our own survival. But when we are relaxed, we can connect with a deeper sense of purpose and our innate altruism. In turn, this supports a healthier relationship to ourselves and to the world around us. The more we can experience this level of ease and peace in our minds, the greater the positive effect will be on our whole physiology.

supportive steps in the seven step programme
Each step of the programme contains an exercise called Inner Conscious Relaxation (ICR), which is adapted from the techniques used in yoga. It is a method of achieving deep relaxation which has been practised for thousands of years. Through it you will become more at ease within yourself, entering a state of all-embracing oneness.

developing the **relaxed** mind

As we have seen, the stress response is dependent on our perceptions, attitudes and beliefs. The power of thought is such that if we think we are getting stressed or overwhelmed, we are more likely to induce the stress response; if we think easeful and relaxing thoughts, we will bring about the relaxation response. These two different ways of being significantly affect the way in which we communicate and conduct our relationships with others. For instance, in a stressed state we can get irritated or overwhelmed by relatively small events, such as a child interrupting our conversation or a colleague being late for a meeting. In a relaxed state, we can view such disturbances for what they are without letting them affect us negatively. We stay balanced and non-judgemental, more likely to be concerned about what the child might need or the reason why our colleague is late, than focusing on the inconvenience to ourselves.

getting started To activate a relaxation response, start by becoming aware of your reactions, of the ways in which you deal with various situations, and particularly of how and when your stress levels begin to rise. Obvious signs are when your breathing starts to get shorter, you feel a tightness in the abdominal muscles, a headache develops, you get more short-tempered, or you are aware of a growing sense of hopelessness or confusion. If you can focus your awareness on any one of these symptoms, then you can begin to elicit the relaxation response. This is achieved using two distinct techniques.

breathing As the stress response is gaining momentum, find a quiet place to be alone. If possible, lie on the floor, as this will relax your abdominal muscles and allow for deeper breathing, or go outside into the open air. Breathe as deeply as you can, filling from your belly up to your chest, and then let the breath out slowly. Do this at least ten times. If you cannot be alone, do your breathing while others are busy around you, quietly deepening each breath.

positive thinking Learn to watch your thoughts, especially when you can feel the pressure rising. Do your thoughts become more annoyed, self-centred, fearful or helpless? We expend far more energy maintaining a stressed state than we do on creating a relaxed one. For instance, if you invariably react by getting so irritated by being interrupted that you start raising your voice, try taking some deep breaths and then silently repeating to yourself a positive message, such as, 'My work is flowing well. Nothing can disturb that flow. I can easily take a few minutes to attend to other issues.' Or perhaps you are feeling tired at the end of a working day and you have to travel home through heavy traffic. As you start feeling crowded, hostile or even angry, try telling yourself, 'All these people around me are an extension of myself. They are all beautiful, loving souls, doing their best to cope with a busy world.' Feel your heart opening and sending out love to all these people. Visualize that you are all flowing through the congestion, like a sea of love moving as one. It may sound strange, but it works!

Alternatively, you may find you are suffering from growing feelings of inadequacy. In this case, turn your thoughts into dynamic ones, such as, 'I am absolutely capable of fulfilling anything that is asked of me', or, 'I have all the knowledge that I need to do this already inside me', or, 'I am resourceful and fully able to rise to this challenge.'

inner joy The beauty of working with the relaxation response is that, as the inner layers of stress are released, we discover a natural joy within ourselves. Where before there was anxiety or constant nagging thoughts jostling for room in our minds, now there is a delicious, peaceful expansiveness and spaciousness.

It is a marvellous revelation to discover that real happiness lies within us, that it is not dependent on anyone or anything else. We do not have to behave in a certain way, we do not have to be rich, thin, married or successful, we do not have to pay our dues or suffer more in order to be happy. We can touch a level of joy that is unconditional, that knows no limitations or restrictions. Even more of a revelation is that as this happiness does not come from anywhere external, so it must have always been there, inside us, simply waiting for us to connect with it. And it will always be there, a source of innate joy, a richness of spirit, no matter what may be happening in our lives. This happiness is our birthright, a natural expression of our being and we have every right to enjoy it.

soft belly

Find a comfortable place to sit with your back straight and your chest relaxed. Take a full inhalation, filling your lungs as deeply as you can, and as you release it through your mouth, imagine it taking all your tension with it. Breathe deeply and, as you breathe, silently repeat, 'Soft belly, soft belly, soft belly'. As your breath fills your belly let it soften any tension that is there. You cannot remain stressed when your belly is relaxed. Do this three times.

Now come back to your normal breathing and just watch the inhalation and exhalation for a few minutes as the breath enters and leaves your body. Then take another deep breath and this time silently repeat, 'Soft heart, soft heart, soft heart'. Breathe into the area at the centre of your chest – the heartspace – and feel your breath softening any resistance. Breathe out tension, breathe in openness, ease, mercy and compassion. Do this three times, then return to your normal breathing.

Just observe the flow of your natural breath for a few minutes. You can do this at any time, anywhere.

being responsible

We can only move from the stress response to the relaxation response when we decide to take responsibility for ourselves. Pointing a finger at others or at our circumstances and blaming them for our stress only complicates matters, creating more chaos while resolving nothing. When we accept that more often than not our external circumstances are actually a reflection of what is going on inside ourselves, only then will we see that if we want to change our world, we must first start by changing ourselves. To be responsible is to be able to respond to both: to ourselves and our own needs, and to others. This does not meaning putting our own needs before those of anyone else, nor does it mean putting them last. There has to be a balance between acknowledging our own requirements and being able to respond to and care for the other people in our lives. To do this means being responsible for ourselves in relation to others.

This concept of responsibility is very important where close relationships are concerned. Too easily we fall into patterns of guilt or blame, pitting our own needs against those of our partner, demanding that we be heard or attended to but refusing to acknowledge that they also have needs. Or we sacrifice our own feelings in order to make our partner happy, in the belief that we are somehow less important than they are. This can happen in a marriage as much as it can with children, parents or a business partner at work.

As we deepen the relaxation response we begin to make contact with a greater self-acceptance and inner ease. This enables us to deal more effectively with issues such as a lack of self-esteem or confidence, and with guilt, shame or insecurity. We can step back from such concerns and go beneath our normal doubts and preoccupations to a place that is more spacious and loving. We do not have to hold on so tightly to our negative beliefs or perceived inadequacies. We can let go and still be safe.

Applied to our relationships, we find that the more relaxed we are, the more we are able to communicate and behave with greater expansiveness and openness. We can stay in touch with who we are, while at the same time being more attuned to what the other person is feeling and experiencing. We are able to make our own needs known more clearly without denying those of anyone else. The end result is that we respond more effectively and are therefore less likely to react with stress.

supportive steps in the seven step programme

Step ❶ focusses on your relationship to yourself, as this directly influences all your relationships with others. **Step ❷** will enable you to deepen your understanding of your responses to others.

recognizing behavioural patterns

Each day, preferably before you go to bed, spend a few minutes reviewing your reactions to stressors. Make sure that you will be undisturbed, and sit or lie down comfortably. Pay particular attention to those times when you ended up reacting negatively either to yourself or to another, and reflect on how you might be able to change such reactions in the future.

Begin by taking a few deep breaths and feel your body unwind. When you are ready, allow your mind to review the day's events. Watch yourself moving through your day. Observe your reactions, feelings and bodily responses. Can you see where the stress began? What did you find especially difficult, and how did you react? Did you blame the other person? Did you feel unable to cope? Did you get angry or feel hopeless? Did you choose to ignore your feelings? Just fully acknowledge whatever happened.

Now visualize someone who you think of as an emotionally balanced, understanding and loving person. It might be the Buddha or Jesus, a parent, mentor or teacher. Then recall your day's most stressful events again, only this time replace yourself with this other person. How do they respond to these situations, to your screaming children, demanding boss, your need to meet deadlines? Follow through each scenario with this other person, watching how they find a balance and maintain their dignity.

As they have responded, so also can you. It is easy to shrug this off by thinking that you could never be like they are, but we are all capable of being relaxed, wise and loving. If it is inside one of us, then it is inside all of us.

making a commitment

Not having enough time is undoubtedly the most common reason why people do not practise either relaxation or meditation. Trying to put more into an already over-filled schedule can seem impossible, especially if there is no obvious slot into which to fit the quiet time we need to connect with ourselves. Yet this very 'busyness' is usually a sign that taking time for ourselves is precisely what we need to do.

We have to ask ourselves, honestly, if this is how we want to live. For it is very simple – no one can make more time for us, or change our lifestyle, other than ourselves. We are the only ones who can make a commitment to our sanity, to our peace, to a deeper appreciation of life, to our health and happiness. The world will always be full of distractions, of things that need to be done, of demands and expectations. We must learn to take time for ourselves despite all the pressures. The Seven Step Programme does take time – about an hour a day – but the more committed you are to your own well-being the more you will benefit from this.

One of the biggest challenges is how to have guilt-free personal time. Perhaps the easiest way to address this is to observe what happens when we don't take time for ourselves. If you spend each day working or looking after other people's needs, do you get resentful, tired, irritated, short-tempered, upset, or feel uncared for? Do you lose your sense of humour, your patience, tolerance and joy? And, if any of this is true, is it really helping anyone?

Taking time for yourself is not selfish, it is one of the most selfless things you could do. Practising the relaxation response profoundly affects both your attitudes to yourself and to others; it enables you to create a more peaceful, respectful and loving environment that benefits you and all those around you. Instead of others feeling at fault because you are angry or exhausted, you will be able to share quality time together. So by taking time for yourself, you will be able to give others far more than if you were available all the time. Normally we do everything else first and put ourselves last. With relaxation as your priority, your sanity is rightly seen as more important than washing the dishes or making phone calls.

The way to start is by showing a genuine respect for yourself, by really accepting that unless you look after your physical, mental and emotional health, you will be of little use to anyone. A stressed mind will see life as a struggle, as something too overwhelming to cope with; when you take time for yourself, you have the chance to discover life as a wondrous and exciting adventure.

supportive steps in the seven step programme
The entire programme encourages you to discover your commitment to yourself and to your health. Each step takes you into different areas of your life to help you bring that commitment into practice.

commitment to yourself

This exercise will help you see where your real commitments lie and how to bring them alive in your life. Find a quiet place to sit and have some paper and a pen with you. Take a few moments to settle, watching your breath and relaxing your body. When you are ready, ask yourself the following questions:

★ What happens to me when I do not have time to myself?

★ What is the effect of this on other people?

★ Do I resent the amount of things I have to do?

★ How do I list my priorities? Where am I on the list?

★ Do I believe my peace of mind is more important than anything else?

★ Do I want to make a commitment to developing the relaxation response?

★ Have I shared this with my family and asked for their support?

★ How can I change my schedule to accommodate time for myself as a top priority?

★ Am I fully prepared to follow this through?

Ask any other questions you need to so that you can see how to make the changes that are necessary for you to practise the relaxation response in your daily life.

gaining an **overview**

Making friends with who we are, just as we are, is a vital step towards gaining inner peace and happiness. If we cannot be at ease with ourselves, then it will not be possible to be truly at peace with anyone else. Yet so many of us deny our feelings, dislike our bodies, and believe that we are full of faults with few redeeming qualities.

our labels and masks To gain an overview of how we see ourselves, start by doing the *Time Out: Noting and Labelling* exercise opposite. This will enable you to get in touch with all the different labels you use to define who you are. For instance, we identify or label ourselves with our race, or the country in which we were born: I'm English, I'm Afro-American, I'm Jewish from Austria, etc. We also gain a sense of identity through our religion, sometimes feeling a separation from, if not a hostility towards, those who follow a different path.

Our work is another important source of identity. As children we are asked what we want to become when we grow up, the implication being that our work is synonymous with our identity: I'm a doctor, I'm a teacher, I'm a bus driver. If we do not become what

was expected of us, if we do not succeed in fulfilling our early aspirations, we may carry feelings of failure, guilt or unworthiness.

Race, nationality and occupation are the big labels that define, and confine, our identity. Then there are the more personal labels, the many ways in which we see ourselves, such as weak, strong, unworthy, worried, intelligent, stupid, hopeless, critical, and so on. We also have many smaller labels that we wear like masks, in order to hide our real feelings or be thought of in a certain way, such as a nice mask, a sociable mask, a confident or tough mask.

Recognizing all the ways in which we label ourselves and all the masks that we put on is a vital part of our journey to understanding ourselves fully.

Do you switch from one mask or role to another during the day, keeping the real you hidden? Behind the masks, who is there? Do you know this person? Are you really an angry person, or is there also a gentle and loving person inside? Are you really so helpless or so bossy?

What happens when you name the different parts of yourself? Can you see how you identify with the content of your life, while beneath all the labels is your essence? Can you find who is there without the labels, without all the many ways you think you are? We so identify with the images we create that we may lose sight of what lies beneath them. But the labels are only a part of us, not the whole of us, and we need to honour our whole being.

noting and labelling

Find a comfortable place to sit quietly. Have a pen and some paper with you. Start by taking a few deep breaths while you feel your body relaxing and settling.

When you are ready, begin by making a list of all your big labels, the ones that are most obvious, such as race, age, religion, work, parent, child, sibling, and so on. Build a list that would tell the outside world who you are.

Now make a list of all your personal labels, your health, size, looks, beliefs; then your emotional and mental labels – how you see yourself and how you think others see you; then all the ways in which you hide your real self, all the masks you use to present yourself to the world.

Relax for a moment, then look at your lists again. Read them through a few times and see if you can find the real you in amongst the labels. Can you find the you that hides behind the masks? Write down any ideas on how you could bring this more hidden part of you into your life so that you can begin to let go of the labels and the masks. Then take a deep breath and relax!

Keep this list for reference as you continue reading the book.

self-acceptance

If you did the *Time Out* exercise on the last page, you will be more familiar with all the various parts of yourself and how you feel about them. And no doubt you will have also admitted that there are sides to you that you do not feel so good about. Making friends with ourselves means acknowledging everything – both the good and the not so good. Do you honour your feelings, or think of them as silly or unimportant? Do you feel comfortable with your body, or do you wish you were different? If we are to heal the effects of stress in our bodies and our lives, we need to be aware of and accept every part of ourselves. This means seeing ourselves just as we are, not as we would like to be, and noticing how and when we judge our behaviour, looks or feelings as wrong, weak, embarrassing or shameful.

All the ways in which we dismiss our feelings and the judgements we make about ourselves disturb our inner tranquillity. They create tension, conflict, secrecy, fear, mistrust and guilt. In trying to hide how we feel about ourselves, we resist intimacy with others, so that no-one else can really know us. We keep ourselves busy in a desperate attempt to avoid confronting what is going on inside ourselves, or we bury our feelings in the hope that they will somehow disappear. Self-rejection destroys our confidence, self-esteem and creativity – all this because we cannot accept ourselves just as we are.

To compound matters, many of us were brought up to think it is self-centred or immodest to think well of ourselves. Yet self-acceptance is not about being egotistical or self-obsessed. It is about accepting that this is who we are, and that we cannot be like someone else. But what we can do is change our attitude towards ourselves and see that we are unique, and that we have our own special beauty. In the same way, we cannot change a difficult or unhappy past, but we can acknowledge that it has happened and release our negative feelings towards it.

Is a caterpillar less fascinating than a butterfly just because it is physically unattractive? Or is it equally valuable, important and beautiful? When we can accept and even appreciate our beauty as it is, we naturally evolve into a wiser and more loving being. Just as a sweet-smelling rose grows best in manure, all the things within us we found so hard to approve of become the very means by which to develop a deeper acceptance and love for both ourselves and others. Gaining a positive self-image, greater self-esteem and confidence does not mean that we are full of self-importance. Rather, these qualities are the natural by-products of making friends with ourselves.

supportive steps in the seven step programme
In **Step ❶** you will learn to accept who you are and discover a sense of belonging and individuality. In **Steps ❻** and **❼** your intuitive wisdom and a greater sense of personal peace will develop.

Find a comfortable place to sit, breathing deeply and relaxing your body. Now go back to the list you made of all your masks and labels (*Time Out: Noting and Labelling* page 25) – all the different pieces that make up you. Try the following exercise.

Highlight those elements that you feel are particularly unacceptable and then choose one, perhaps the one that feels most pertinent to you today. Allow your mind to explore all your feelings about this part of you: examine its history, how it has affected your life, whether it has limited your relationships, happiness or creativity. Really get to know it.

Now be aware to what extent you are judging this part as unacceptable. See if you can find where these judgemental feelings are coming from. Are they your own feelings or do they come from your parents, partner or society? For a moment see if you can simply suspend or let go of that judgement. Then see how you feel about this part. Do you still want to isolate or reject it? Or without the judgement can you bring it into your heart, to a place of love? Can you see it as an integral part of your being that needs to be embraced and cared for?

Focus on your breathing and with each breath feel your heart opening ever more deeply to accepting yourself just as you are.

overcoming the obstacles

Anxiety, frustration, anger and loneliness are as much a cause of the stress response as they are a by-product of it. Becoming fearful of an impending deadline, for instance, can cause anxiety, lower tolerance levels, and increase a sense of separation or loneliness. These states present serious obstacles to achieving any peace of mind.

fear and anxiety As we saw earlier, a certain amount of fear or apprehension is normal, and even necessary, in certain circumstances; for example, fear that arises in the face of danger is a natural and protective response. Each time we enter into a new or unknown situation — our first day at school, taking examinations, being interviewed for a job — both fear and excitement will accompany us, our minds and bodies alert and ready. But when fear turns to anxiety it acts as an anaesthetic, numbing our deeper feelings and paralysing us from moving forwards. Anxiety is based on the *possibility* of something happening, on the *thought* of being wrong or incompetent, or on an *imagined* negative outcome. When such unfounded fears occur frequently they will continually undermine our confidence, personal power and capabilities.

frustration Frustration arises in response to feelings of powerlessness, when circumstances become out of our control, such as when we are stuck in a traffic jam on the way to an important meeting. We may also feel frustrated in relation to others, towards a teenage daughter who stays out later than requested, for example. We feel helpless and obstructed when our desires are thwarted; what we may fail to see is how our fears and frustration colour our perception and prevent our ability to stay calm.

anger Stress-related anger and irritation arise when our expectations have not been fulfilled, or when other people act or events happen in a way that we perceive as being a hindrance or a provocation.

When we feel unable to perform or cope we may give vent to sudden outbursts of rage with little apparent justification — how easily we blame others for our own feelings of inadequacy! We are convinced that the actions of others are responsible for our feelings, when in fact no one can actually make us angry — the anger is with ourselves, not anyone else.

loneliness Isolation and loneliness can occur even if we are surrounded by people. We tell ourselves that no-one else can understand, that nobody can do what has to be done but us. If we persist with such beliefs, we can become more and more isolated, rejecting all help. We lose touch with our ability to share and care; we fail to see that we are not friendless, that there are others who are willing to help and to hold us.

In the face of such obstacles it is essential to develop the relaxation response, in order to save our sanity, let alone our health and happiness. These same barriers to our well-being can be turned into stepping stones that lead to greater self-understanding. In a relaxed state, fear and anxiety are replaced by fearlessness and confidence; they become the motivating forces to enter into a deeper understanding of ourselves. Frustration is replaced by trust, a confidence that allows events to unfold in their own way. Anger is replaced by patience and tolerance, the ability to be more open to other ways of being. Loneliness is replaced by a willingness to embrace others and to communicate with them.

turning obstacles into stepping stones

This exercise can be done with frustration, anger or any other emotional state as the focus. We have chosen to start with anxiety as it is often the most debilitating of all. The aim is to develop a greater awareness of how and when anxiety arises, and how it influences your behaviour, thoughts or feelings. As this awareness deepens, you will find that you feel less like a victim. Anxiety loses its power when we turn to face it.

For one whole week you need to become an observer of your fears or anxiety. Carry a note pad and pen with you. Whenever you feel anxiety arising, observe what happens. Then ask yourself these questions:

★ What was happening before the fear arose? What triggered the anxiety? Was it a particular circumstance, a person, or a thought or feeling inside you?

★ What effect did your anxiousness have on you physically? Note any physical changes, such as getting hot or cold, sweating, palpitations, stomach cramp, headache, etc.

★ What effect did the anxiety have on you mentally and emotionally? Did you become nervous, weepy, frightened, helpless, powerless, overwhelmed, etc?

★ What followed the anxiety? Did frustration, anger or any other state arise?

★ How long did the anxiety last? How long did it take to come back to a relaxed state?

After a few days of doing this, note if your responses are changing, if anxiety is arising less often, or if you feel able to cope with it better. Watch what happens to anxiety when you are no longer fearful of it.

the **courage** to change

Developing a relaxed mind involves creating a lifestyle to support it. Making changes to our routine is essential, and this is often the hardest part. We tend to be very attached to our way of being, even if it is detrimental to our physical, mental or emotional health. The old patterns are comfortable and familiar, whereas change can seem unknown or beyond us.

How many times have you said, 'I must do more exercise,' or 'I must stop getting so angry,' but never reach the point of actually doing it? Inside, we know where we need to implement changes, but making them always seems to belong to some other place or time: 'When I go on holiday I will really relax,' or 'I can start doing yoga after the children have left for school.' And how often do you long to make changes yet feel constrained by commitments to work, family or the needs of others? How often has guilt stopped you from taking time for yourself?

Letting go of the old and the familiar often requires us to dig a bit deeper to discover which of our beliefs and attitudes are holding us back from making real changes. We acquire many of our life views and bad habits during the early part of our lives; we learn directly from our parents and teachers, often adopting their ideas about religion, race, sex, money, work, relationships, even the meaning of life. It is through them that we discover the world and how to play our part in it. In this way, we are moulded and conditioned by the generations that have gone before us. It is important to recognize this so that we become less attached to some of the more unhelpful ideas we

have acquired, and to explore what we truly think and feel. As we get older we begin to form our own opinions and beliefs, but it is not always easy to express these, especially if it means going against the grain.

Change is the essence of life. If we resist change we cannot live life fully. We become stuck, entrenched in the past, fixed in old ways. The same life force that enables a weed to grow through a thick slab of concrete to reach daylight is in us too. It is the life force that constantly seeks fulfilment, inner peace and happiness. When we put off change we are putting life on hold; when we have the courage to try new ways of being we are embracing life. Rather than blaming our parents or guardians for having passed their prejudiced or confused views on to us, we can be grateful that we now have the awareness to change such limited views.

Awareness itself is transformative. As you begin to see your entrenched patterns of thinking and behaving, they will lose their power over you. You will learn to discriminate between those beliefs and attitudes that enhance your life and those that are outmoded; to honour your own desire for something new, however different it may appear from your conditioning. Change brings fresh possibilities and new awakenings.

supportive steps in the seven step programme
Throughout the programme we suggest lifestyle changes, such as modifications to your diet and attitude, so that you can experience different ways of doing things until you find what feels best for you.

making changes

This exercise will help you to see where you are holding on to old and unhelpful ways of being. You need to become an observer of yourself for at least one week and keep a daily journal. At the end of each day take a moment to reflect on the day's events and your responses, and particularly on those areas where you feel change is needed. Observe and note your reactions, attitudes, behaviour and resistances.

Do your thoughts and actions actually reflect how you feel, or can you see where you are reacting out of old patterns, perhaps in ways that your mother or father did? Make a note of where you felt your responses did not express the real you. See if you can recognize from where or whom those responses were coming.

For instance, perhaps your parents instilled in you a strong belief that it is important to succeed, that you have to work hard and push yourself to be the very best. As a result you have succeeded – but at a price. You have little time to be with your family and your health is suffering. Whenever you want to take time off you feel guilty because you believe you are not trying hard enough.

Now ask yourself how differently you would approach a particular issue in your life if you were following your own ideas or feelings. What would you say? What would you do? Breaking the moulds of old patterns may feel a little threatening at first; there can be an uncertainty about who you are or how you should behave. But there is also a tremendous feeling of liberation, as if letting go of a great weight or burden.

from me to you

Relationships give meaning, purpose and joy to our lives, whether they are relationships with our immediate family and friends, or with our colleges at work. However, our relationship to ourselves colours and influences any communication we have with others. Too often, our unacknowledged expectations or needs put pressure on this communication, and so finding a more profound level of happiness within ourselves is essential if we are to maintain successful relationships. This is a different quality of happiness from one we may have experienced before, as it is not dependent on anyone or anything outside of us.

finding happiness

Our normal view of happiness is that it lies somewhere in the future. We tell ourselves that we will be happy when we have more money, an ideal partner, a better job, when our children are married, or when we get well. The present seems to lack a sense of real satisfaction, so we dream of a time to come when we will finally be fulfilled.

But if happiness does come do we trust it fully? Many of us have been hurt, let down or have had to struggle through difficult times, and our ability to trust that happiness can last has been destroyed. We are used to life being stressful, even painful. This makes us fearful of trusting the good times: we do not believe happiness will stay but that some new difficulty will soon follow. Happiness is seen as something transient, impermanent or unreliable.

We may also have a hard time believing that we deserve happiness. Guilt and shame colour our behaviour – either the guilt that says we cannot be happy until we have redeemed our sins, or the shame that buries our happiness inside. We believe that we have to earn happiness or pay for it in some way, that happiness is bestowed from a source outside ourselves in response to our own behaviour.

What we discover through the relaxation response is that as the inner layers of stress and guilt are released they reveal a spaciousness, like letting into a gentle quiet that allows genuine joy. As peace fills your being, so does happiness, coming together in natural partnership as we let go of the stress.

You will see the effect of this in your relationships with all those around you, for although each one of us is primarily responsible for ourselves, for finding that place inside that is accepting and at ease – and for making the changes that support this – we do not exist in isolation. Relationships are fundamental to our existence. Whether we live alone or with others, we are all in relationship of one form or another – to each other, to our immediate environment and to the physical world beyond. Everything we do, think or feel affects all those around us in many different ways.

stress and relationships

When we are more deeply connected to the happiness inside ourselves, all our relationships will benefit, for stress both affects and is affected by our communication and interaction with others. For instance, arguments or misunderstandings with a partner can be caused by rising stress levels, perhaps because of difficulties at work, a family crisis or financial strain; alternatively, if a relationship is becoming more conflictive, this in turn will become a debilitating stressor.

Supportive emotional relationships, both at home and at work, make an enormous difference to our ability to deal with stress or crisis. They provide a safe place, one in which we can be sure of finding comfort and reassurance. Any disruption to that foundation invariably makes it harder to cope – separation, divorce and loneliness are up at the top of the list of stress-producing situations.

finding an open heart As relationships are so vital to our well-being, and as stress can have such an adverse affect on them, we need to be aware of the importance of being open and honest with those who are closest to us. If we ignore or deny our feelings, then not only are we being insincere and avoiding intimacy, but we are also creating more stress within ourselves. Repressed feelings do not just disappear – they stay locked inside, influencing our attitudes and behaviour. For instance, feelings of being misunderstood or not trusted turn into resentment; resentment turns into arguments, conflict and, finally, distress or even depression.

Awareness is the key here. We need to see from where these feelings arise, why they affect us so deeply, and how we can bring about a peaceful resolution. Being honest about our feelings and respecting both our own emotional life and the experiences of others is essential if we are to develop greater maturity and love.

being together There cannot be intimacy in a relationship until we let go of our defences and allow the other to see us as we really are: intimacy – *into me*

you see. True intimacy with others cannot occur unless we are willing to be intimate with ourselves – to accept and embrace ourselves as we are. Only then will we not be fearful of being seen by another. When we are feeling at ease with ourselves, intimacy is wonderful: it enables us to go into a depth of sharing and caring with another that dissolves the ego boundaries. But when stress levels are rising, intimacy can make us feel as if we have no personal space, that there is nowhere we can go to be private, no room for our own thoughts. We want to shut out the world, and that includes those who are closest to us. It takes great effort to let go of the fears and inadequacies that isolate us, and be willing to reconnect with our innate loving nature.

being alone Spending time alone gives us the chance to be in more direct relationship to ourselves, to learn about and make friends with ourselves, to experience the depth of oneness with all life, to be alone, or 'at one with all'. This is a rich, vibrant and essential experience that some people seek through the solitude of retreat.

Loneliness is not the same as being alone. Loneliness is when we consciously isolate and separate ourselves from others. Where loneliness contracts and pulls in, sharing and caring in relationships expands outwards, opening our hearts to the world beyond our immediate concerns. As we break through the walls of separation surrounding us, we discover that we are all interconnected, that we each have a profound intimacy with all life.

supportive steps in the seven step programme
As you practise the meditation and relaxation exercises in each step, you will find your sense of self changing, bringing you to greater self-understanding. This naturally gives rise to more open and loving relationships.

open communication

Communication is an essential life skill. Through it we expand our understanding, go beyond our separate selves into the hearts of others, and know that we are a part of something much greater than ourselves. Without communication we have wars, families become dysfunctional, loneliness increases, marriages break down, stress levels rise. Just through the tone of your voice and the words you speak you can increase intimacy, safety and love; conversely, you can cause hurt, rejection and conflict. How often have you felt that you were not being heard? How often do you actually listen to what someone is saying? And do you listen without judging or criticizing? Do you and your partner or children take time just to talk together, expressing your feelings and really hearing each other?

Communication is about sharing our story or our feelings as much as it is taking in what someone else is saying or being listened to by others – being received and heard. It is a two-way experience and both sides are equally important: an honesty in communicating and an openness in receiving. Talking without being fully heard creates deep frustration, resentment and isolation, or feelings of being unrecognized and unworthy.

When stress levels are rising, we stop being able to listen. There is no room inside us for anyone or anything else, we are filled to the brim with ourselves and our troubles. Yet it is precisely at times like these, when the stress response needs to be released, that a deeper and more meaningful communication with others is required.

Even at the best of times, many of us find communication difficult because we don't know how to express our feelings. As children we may not have been encouraged to share our hopes or fears, but were taught to keep our feelings to ourselves, to suffer in silence. Perhaps our parents never really communicated their feelings, so we did not learn how to do this, or perhaps we were never really listened to, so we simply closed down. In later life we may feel

embarrassed, or even threatened or exposed, if we share our feelings, as if a secret hiding place has been revealed. With limitations such as these it is difficult to know what we really feel, to get in touch with the deeper currents that flow through our hearts. However, the more we share – even if it is hard at first – the less threatening it will become, and the more we will feel deeply connected to ourselves and to others. As we find our voice, so it will grow stronger, also helping others to find theirs.

Far from feeling exposed, it is a great relief to be intimately known and accepted by another, to be fully received. Rather than being locked inside, alone with our feelings, someone else knows us and can share both our problems and our joy. We no longer have to carry our story around with us, constantly affirming it by repeating it to everyone we encounter; we can safely put it down and focus on the story others have to tell. To truly listen to another is an essential part of communication – to receive them into ourselves without judgement or criticism, without trying to make everything right or to heal or fix a problem, without getting defensive or feeling we are at fault, but simply being there in companionship.

communicating together

Communication is so important in our lives that we need to create a special time when we do nothing else. This exercise is for two people. One person simply listens as the other one speaks, then they reverse roles, and after both have spoken there is time for feedback and discussion. Start with 15 minutes of talking for each person, followed by 15 minutes' discussion, although you can lengthen this time if you want to. If you are doing this to help solve relationship difficulties, then use the feedback time to work constructively with the issues that have been raised. The object is to be open to both sharing and listening.

Sit opposite your partner, either on chairs or on the floor. Decide who will go first. The one who is speaking can say whatever they want, with as much honesty and openness as possible. The more you do this, the clearer your feelings will be. The one who is listening pays full attention and listens with an open heart. No feedback, no interruption. No judgement, no defensiveness, no fixing. Just listening. After you have both spoken, then, with awareness, share your insights together.

Try to do this exercise at least once a week. It can also be done with more than two people, letting each person speak before feedback. During the feedback, only one person should speak at a time.

tenderheartedness

The more the mind relaxes, the more the heart can open. As we move from a stressed state to a relaxed one, we are also moving towards a tender heart, one that is capable of generosity, loving kindness, compassion, forgiveness and mercy. We move from an unhealthy or negative relationship to ourselves to a healthy and positive one, where these more altruistic qualities become a natural response to both ourselves and others.

Being generous invariably benefits the giver more than it does the receiver: there is nothing quite like witnessing the joy in another's face. Giving to someone else is especially powerful if we are feeling bereft, lacking in some way, or fearful of not having enough. It enables us to go beyond our limitations and share our humanness, our loving heart. This is a very precious gift. Even if you think you have nothing to offer, you can always give a smile or a kind word.

Loving kindness and compassion may seem very lofty qualities to aim for, but they are naturally within us. Deep inside we know that we have the capacity for great love, for a caring that goes beyond our individual needs. You may have experienced this at the birth of a child, or at a time of extreme difficulty such as when a natural disaster strikes and people put their own needs aside to help others. But we do not need a disaster in order to be more caring, we can begin now.

Thinking only of ourselves tends to isolate us and create deep loneliness. As soon as you open your heart to love you will feel uplifted and deeply connected. This is not always as easy as it sounds. At times you may feel as if the doors to your heart are stiff and rusty from having been closed too long; pushing them open may be painful – but it can be done.

Forgiveness cannot be separated from love; it arises as a natural expression of the heart. Forgiveness does not mean that we must ignore the hurt we have received nor accept what was done to us. But we can forgive the person responsible for our pain if we can recognize that they acted out of fear, hurt and confusion. Once we can accept that we are all human, we see that we are all capable of making mistakes, of hurting each other. The reason forgiveness is so powerful is that it releases the hurt and suffering that keeps us in such distress. When we are feeling angry or vengeful, we lose touch with our deepest heart. Not being able to forgive only creates further suffering within us. When we can forgive it is like a dam being opened, it releases a flow of loving and healing energies that makes us whole again. Forgiveness is a greater gift to ourselves than it is to others.

supportive steps in the seven step programme
Step ❹ contains a meditation called Loving Kindness, which will enable you to let go of resistance so that love and compassion can permeate every part of your being. In **Step ❺** the Forgiveness Meditation will enable you to develop greater levels of mercy and acceptance.

generosity, kindness and forgiveness

This is a four-day exercise. On Day One make a point of saying hello or smiling at people — both strangers and those you know — and watch what happens. See if it changes how you feel, or if it changes them. Give something beautiful to someone. As you do this, watch if fear arises or if fear separates you from sharing. See if the more you give the more you get.

On Day Two spend the whole day being kind and generous to yourself. Honour your own needs, watching those times you ignore your feelings and practising even greater generosity at those moments. On Day Three be kind to people you meet — practise random acts of kindness wherever you go.

Then try practising forgiveness on Day Four. Forgiving ourselves is just as important as forgiving others, so each time either yourself or someone else does something that is annoying or hurtful, take a deep breath and silently repeat, 'I forgive you'. Watch what happens to your feelings. The quicker you can forgive, the quicker you will release your distress and find an inner peace.

being versus doing

How we feel about our work has an enormous effect on our state of mind, health and stress levels. If we are happy with our vocation, we are more likely to be content and fulfilled, to look after our health and have more energy for other activities. We are unlikely to get stressed or feel overworked. However, if we are not happy with what we are doing, our lack of fulfilment can easily turn into resentment and jealousy, leading to ill-health, marital problems, low stress tolerance and tiredness – a deep inner exhaustion that is like fighting an uphill battle.

Finding fulfilment at work does not necessarily mean changing our job (although it may do), but it does require changing our attitude towards what we are doing and where we are going. We need to be realistic about our needs and desires, and have goals that are appropriate – career aims that are a little beyond our grasp, perhaps, but that are definitely within our reach. To aim too high is only going to cause distress.

At the same time, instead of seeing them as hindrances, we need to view the frustrations of our current situation as opportunities to grow in patience, tolerance, compassion, assertiveness and creativity. When we see that the world is not our enemy, that it is there to help us evolve beyond our own limitations, we can accept that there is something to be learnt from every situation. To be content with our work does not mean that we have to be the best; it is enough to be at ease with ourselves and to enjoy whatever we do. This inspires motivation, perseverance and greater vision.

We shouldn't deny our dreams and aspirations, however. What happened to the child longing to work with animals, to be an opera singer, or to drive a fire engine? Is there one ambition that you still long to fulfil, if not as a career then as a hobby? What would you need to do now to begin to make your dream come true? Do you need to go to an evening class or college? Is it something for which you can volunteer, or do you need to join a club or association?

Discovering what we really want to do with our lives involves more than just making a career choice. It is about finding a deeper purpose, a reason for being, so that our work becomes an expression of who we really are. Connecting with that deeper meaning gives us the strength to cope. We know that our happiness is not dependent on what we do and, if change occurs, we can flow with it while staying true to ourselves. This is especially important if we face redundancy, financial loss or a shift in our lifestyle.

In the same vein, we tend to be aware of what we are doing so much that we forget about being. Each is essential for our mental and emotional well-being, but often 'doing' takes the upper hand. We put so much energy into doing that we lose touch with the ability just to be: to feel our own presence, to appreciate the rain drops on a leaf, to watch the sun go down, to communicate with our loved ones. Are you so caught up in business or achievement that you have no time to walk barefoot in damp grass, to dance or to sing? Can you see where you need to bring more balance into your life?

See how a rose is so vibrant and smells so sweet? Yet it does not smell any different if it is unnoticed – it is simply being itself, and that is the gift of its beauty.

discovering purpose

This exercise is to help you focus on your inner purpose and to allow it to manifest itself more readily in your life. Find a quiet place to sit and have paper and a pen with you. Start by breathing deeply and relaxing your body. As you ask yourself the following questions, let your answers arise spontaneously. Take your time with each question.

★ What has most meaning for me in life?

★ When do I feel happiest?

★ When do I feel most fulfilled?

★ Is this my deepest purpose in life? If not, then what is?

★ What needs to change in my life so that I can express my purpose?

★ What is stopping me from doing this now?

★ What one thing can I start now that will enable my greater purpose to manifest itelf?

Allow yourself to think over these questions so that you begin to see a way of moving into a place of deeper expression and meaning.

appreciating our world

When we are stressed we can lose touch with the world around us. We no longer see the beauty and vibrancy of nature, we forget about caring for our environment. Have you ever noticed that if you are in a really good mood, you will go out of your way to pick up rubbish, for instance, or take the trouble to get a spider out of the bath, whereas if you are in a bad mood you will walk past the rubbish or quickly flush the spider down the drain? When we are in a hurry or feel pressured, we are no longer able to appreciate the preciousness and beauty of this world.

Relating to our environment is vital for maintaining our sense of balance and wholeness. We are not isolated entities, but an integral part of a much larger picture, each of us connected to the other, to the earth, oceans and sky, the animals, plants and seasons. Our healing must also include healing our relationship to the physical world. The earth sustains and supports us, the animals feed us, the plants nourish us, the seasons allow all things to grow in their right time. To ignore our world is to deny our roots, our source of life, and serves only to separate us further from ourselves.

Appreciating the natural world has the most wonderful effect on our state of mind. Try making the environment your main focus for a day. Take time to enjoy nature. Walk in a park and smell the flowers or freshly cut grass, notice the patterns of a spider's web filled with rain drops, plant a window box with pansies, geraniums or daffodils to brighten your view.

Find ways that you can contribute to a safer and healthier planet. It is easy to be overwhelmed by the immensity of what needs to be done to help the earth, to save the rainforests, the ozone layer, the oceans and even our own neighbourhood from pollution, over-development or destruction. But ignoring these issues, or hoping that the problems will go away, solves nothing – it simply creates more problems. We must become part of the solution and active participants in our future. Even small gestures can make a big difference. Try to pick up any rubbish you see on the ground; arrange boxes at home or at work for recycling paper, glass and cans; leave your car at home and travel by public transport or arrange car-pooling with others; take your own shopping bags to the supermarket. Think of other ways in which you can contribute to a better world.

The pain of the earth is no different to our own pain. It is the pain of not being loved, cared for, respected or honoured. When we bring healing to the environment it awakens our sense of relatedness and compassion for all life. It expands us beyond ourselves and our immediate concerns, difficulties or pressures. When we embrace our world, we connect more deeply with ourselves.

from chaos to order The way we live and the environment that we create are vital components of our ability to cope with stress. Our home and work surroundings are a reflection of our state of mind – they are like a mirror, an expression of our individuality and personality. It is therefore important to make these as stress-free and nourishing as possible. Take a moment to look around your home. Is it full

case history

There is a lovely story of a child who was getting bored. His father, trying to think of something for him to do, found a picture of the world and tore it into small pieces. He told his son to put the world back together again, thinking this would take him some hours, as the world is a very complicated image. However, the boy finished very quickly. When his father asked him how he had managed to do it so easily, the child explained that there was a picture of a human being on the other side of the paper. When he put the human back together, so the world was put together.

of clutter? Or is everything neatly in its place? Does it feel peaceful or chaotic? Do the same with your work space. Does it feel conducive to working? Is it light and comfortable? Order is important: it forms the foundation from which all things can emerge. Nature is absolutely orderly – the seasons, the tides, the moon and the sun all keep to their ordained path. And yet all this order is not restrictive – it produces the most perfectly spontaneous, outrageously beautiful, creatively wild and fabulously abundant world!

clearing the decks Clutter is like the excess mental energy that fills the mind and unnecessary worries; it can make us feel extra tired, as if there is no room for anything more in our lives. Clearing clutter creates a spaciousness in which we can move freely and creatively. It lifts our spirits and presents greater possibilities. See if you can tidy as you go along, or have a good clear-up once or twice a week, and see if that also creates more space in your mind.

On the other hand, an environment that is excessively neat and tidy can reflect a mind that shuts away feelings, that represses imagination and spontaneity, and holds back from sharing and expression. A desk that is too orderly reflects a mind that does what it is told, but may not be finding its own forms of creativity or originality. While clutter represents chaos, excessive neatness suggests an over-concern with control.

Our homes and work spaces can reflect nature by creating a natural order where each thing has its place. When it is in that place it is of benefit to its whole surroundings. Let each room reflect its purpose and the objects in it mirror each other. Try moving your furniture into a new position, or using different lighting. Bring beauty into your life by having fresh flowers and plants in your home, and throw open windows as much as possible. The more we can bring peace and harmony into our physical surroundings, the more deeply relaxed we will feel being there.

supportive steps in the seven step programme
Step ❷ includes a Nature Walk and an Appreciation Meditation so that you can deepen your relationship to your world.

the path of awareness

a journey of
self-discovery

By now you are probably aware that you are beginning a journey. It may feel as if you are going from being on automatic pilot to taking control of the craft; or as if you are waking up from a long, oblivious sleep. And in a way this *is* what is happening. When we begin to realize that we have choices, that we do not have to be so stressed, that we can make changes in our lives and live with greater joy and happiness, then we are awakening to a different way of being.

However, as with any journey, we need to make the right preparations, to have some idea of where we are going and what we will need. That is the purpose of this book. What will happen is unique to each one of us, for we all have our own journey. No doubt the path will have many twists and turns, it will wander off in all sorts of directions, at times we may even think we have lost sight of it altogether. But each time we come back to ourselves, we rediscover our purpose and direction.

Two of the biggest obstacles we have to deal with are our own doubting mind and the resistance we meet in other people. In the face of these, it is tempting to slide back into old ways of being, to doubt that we are really making any progress, to think that we are not capable of changing, or that we do not have enough time or energy. But we do. There is always enough time for whatever we want to do — always. We have to remind ourselves of our commitment, that we are making this journey to gain greater sanity, not to cause more stress. It is very important to see the progress you are making, rather than feel hopeless about how far there is still to go. Every so often, look back at who you were when you started the programme and it will give you great encouragement. Appreciate your efforts and rejoice in this progress.

The obstacles we encounter from other people are usually over such things as changes in schedule or our need to have time alone. They may also criticize or make fun of us. Any change can be a threat to another's security — there is always a desire to stay with the familiar and known. It is important to talk through why you are wanting to change, how you need to find time to relax and be quiet so that you will have more to give to them. Share your feelings and what you hope to achieve. When they see the difference it makes to your ways of being they may even want to join you.

This is a journey of self-discovery. Most of us start from a place of exhaustion or burn-out. We have had enough of stress and want to reconnect with our lost dreams, our forgotten joys. We want to remember how to live life fully, as lovingly, caringly and peacefully as we can. Part Two leads you through the different practices and lifestyle changes that will support your journey: how to relax and meditate, how to move the body and calm the mind, how to transform old thinking patterns and ways of being — these are the processes we use and the journey unfolds on its own.

journeying

This is a creative visualization (see page 50 for more details) to reconnect you with your journey. You can do it lying down or sitting in a chair. Spend a few minutes breathing and relaxing your body. Then bring your awareness to the area of your heart – the heartspace – and breathe into that area. Try to stay here throughout the practice.

When you are ready, bring into your heart an image of yourself as a baby. Recognize the people around you and remember your home. Slowly continue this process from babyhood, remembering yourself as you grew through being a young child, going to school, then becoming a teenager. Remember the events in your life, your family, your teachers, your friends, the special things you liked to do. Remember what it felt like to be you.

Then slowly continue through your teenage years into young adulthood. Remember the people and places, the yearnings and unfulfilled dreams. Remember how it felt inside, amid all the confusion and growing.

Continue through your adulthood, remembering the events, the decisions you made, the times when everything seemed to flow, and the times when it seemed hard or rocky. Can you see your spirit longing for the light?

Bring yourself up to the present moment. As you do so, see the thread that has strung your life into a whole. The beads on the thread are all the different things that have happened to you, and they have all led to this point. You have been on a journey all along and it will continue. Now you have the chance to choose where you are going.

the importance of breathing

When demands become overwhelming and stress levels are rising, the first place this will show is in the breath. Our breathing becomes faster and more shallow, concentrated only in the upper part of the chest. The way we breathe corresponds directly to the way we feel – happiness, sadness, anger or fear, all have their different type of breath. We normally breathe unconsciously – the lungs function without our conscious intervention – but we can also breathe with conscious awareness. By consciously changing the tempo of our breath from shallow intakes to breaths taken deep in the belly, we can change our emotional state from tension or nervousness to one of being relaxed, centred and at ease. Deep breathing is also helpful in coping with pain or trauma. It is natural to tense against pain, but deep breathing will release our resistance so that the pain becomes less overwhelming.

breath meditation Most spiritual traditions use concentration on the breath as the foundation of their relaxation and meditation techniques. Breathing with awareness brings our attention inwards so that we are less distracted by any external stimuli. Staying in touch with the natural in and out flow of the breath is very grounding, it centres us in the body and enables us to be fully present in the moment. The rhythm of the breath is also that of the seasons, the tides, the sun and the moon – through the breath all living creatures are interconnected.

The simplest form of breath meditation is done by sitting upright and watching the movement of the inhalation and the exhalation. In this gentle way we enter into deeper states of absorption, self-awareness and understanding. As you grow in awareness, the breath becomes an anchor, holding you in the present. At first it is quite natural to find you are breathing erratically, or faster or slower than normal. It is not always easy to watch an unconscious process without wanting to control it, but all you need do is observe its natural flow. After a while your breathing will settle down and you will feel as if you are merging with it. Just breathe one breath at a time, staying with the flow of the breath and the sensation in your body.

During your day, come back to your breathing as often as you can. Even consciously breathing for one, two or three breaths will help you let go of any stress. Your breath is your best friend, dependable and always there to be used to access greater calm.

supportive steps in the seven step programme
Steps ❸ and **❼** include variations of Breath Awareness Meditation, which will lead you progressively through this very important technique.

the practice of **relaxation**

Each step of the programme starts with a relaxation method known as Inner Conscious Relaxation (ICR). This powerful technique has its roots in the teachings of Indian yoga, a system of profound relaxation that has been practised for thousands of years. Through deep relaxation you will ease unconscious layers of tension and enter a profoundly peaceful state. As this can take a while to develop, each ICR practice is designed to extend you further as you progress through each step. In this way you will gain a strong foundation in the technique so that you can continue on your own after completing the programme.

inner conscious relaxation Inner Conscious Relaxation (ICR) begins and ends with repeating a resolve: a short affirmation clarifying our deeper purpose or intent. Affirmations are a way of shifting deeply held and unhealthy ways of thinking or behaving and imprinting positive, healthy ones. When a resolve stays only in the conscious mind, it is easy to give in to conflicting desires. Combining your resolve with ICR takes it deeper into the unconscious, where it works on our unspoken and unseen blocks. It is important that your resolve is right for you, as the aim is to work with it until it becomes an integrated part of your daily life. Let it be a reflection of your innermost heart's desire. (For suggested affirmations see page 49.)

After making the resolve, you continue ICR by moving your consciousness systematically and with awareness through each part of the body. As you silently name each part you also try to visualize it in your mind's eye. In this way, mind and body relax together on a very deep level. This systematic approach is important, as it is by rotating our awareness through the body that we are able to stimulate the relaxation response so completely. Consequently, it is included in every practice.

As you practise ICR, you will be asked to imagine different states, such as the opposites of hot and cold, or light and heavy. Or you may be asked to focus on the space between the body and the floor, bringing awareness to the smallest point of contact. This enables the sensory aspect of the brain to relax and become fully focused.

Visualizations are also utilized in ICR (see also pages 50–51). These help to release negative impressions stored in the unconscious mind, and to replace them with healing and loving images, creating a profound sense of well-being and inner joy. Different images are used in each step of the programme.

During ICR you maintain a stream of unbroken awareness. Your eyes are closed, and your attention is in the space between sleep and wakefulness. In this way you will relax most deeply and will finish your ICR feeling more refreshed than after many hours of sleep.

It is important not to judge your relaxation. It does not matter if you are unable to relax, if you just lie there thinking for the whole session, or even if you fall asleep. Be patient. The idea is not for you to become tense because you cannot relax! Give it time, and gradually you will find that you are becoming calmer and more at ease with less and less effort.

positive thinking and affirmations

An affirmation is a positively worded statement that endorses ourselves and our basic goodness. So often we reinforce our weaknesses, failings or faults by saying things like, 'I'm no good at this', 'I'm always so hopeless', or, 'I'm always getting angry', which only serve to instil even greater hopelessness or anger. The more we confirm our negative states – constantly putting ourselves down, undermining our capabilities and worthiness – the more unhappy we become. You can see this for yourself very easily. When you next come home from work, say to yourself, 'It's been a long day and I'm really tired, I have no energy to do anything.' Do this a few times and observe how you feel. Then try saying, 'It's been a good day, I am feeling energized and ready to play with the kids/go for a walk/cook a lovely dinner.' Do this a few times and watch how you change. Be aware of how, just by shifting your thought patterns, you can completely transform your energy levels and feel much better in yourself.

Affirmations are not meant to deny reality: they are not saying that everything is wonderful when obviously it is not. They simply help us to move out of repetitive and negative mental patterns to find a healthier, more creative approach to all the difficulties that hold us in destructive or critical mind-sets. An affirmation will not take away the cause of your stress, but it will help you deal with stress in a more constructive way. The affirmation reminds you that you are basically good, sane and healthy, that you really are a loving, patient, caring person, and that you are not a victim but are strong and capable.

In repeating an affirmation you are confirming that you are committed really to caring about yourself, and that you no longer want to continue being stressed or tired, or feeling that you are unworthy or unloving. Rather than staying stuck in old ways or sinking even deeper into self-pity, despair or indifference, you are taking action and willing a new and positive direction in your thinking. The body does not know the difference between a real threat or an imagined one: in the dark, a coil of rope that looks like a snake will produce the same stress response as a real one – it is our *perception* that determines the response. By changing our mind-set we change our viewpoint, making healing possible.

When you repeat the same affirmation over a period of time, those places where you get stuck will become clearer. The behaviour that undermines you is highlighted because it now goes against the behaviour you are affirming. For instance, if you are affirming that you are a loving and caring person, then you will see more quickly and honestly the times when you start to behave in an uncaring way.

An affirmation energizes and motivates the unconscious mind to make greater changes than we consciously believe possible. Making such a declaration is a way of asserting our strengths, values and purpose.

It cuts through the conditioned behaviour that may have hampered our growth and connects us with our genuine self.

When you create an affirmation, make it realistic and simple. It does not work to try to change everything at once, or even to work on more than one or two issues at a time. Focus on your immediate priority and start there. It should be a positive statement, such as: 'I am fully relaxed and capable', rather than 'I am no longer stressed', or, 'I am strong and fearless', rather than 'I am no longer fearful'. Make it short and clear, so that it is easy to remember, and keep it in the present tense – 'I am filled with energy and joy', not 'I will be filled with energy and joy' – or you may be putting off your goal indefinitely. Repeat the affirmation as often as you like.

Listed below are some more suggestions for affirmations, but we do urge you to create your own.

I am a fully loving and caring person.

With every breath I am more at peace.

I am flowing through my day with ease.

May loving kindness and compassion fill my heart.

I am awakening my highest potential.

I am deepening my awareness and sensitivity.

May my actions benefit all beings.

supportive steps in the seven step programme

Throughout the programme we suggest affirmations to accompany the theme of each step, although it is preferable to think of your own.

visualization and imagery

The thoughts and images we hold in our minds are very powerful – so powerful that our bodies will respond to them as if they are real. If you believe that you cannot cope, are fearful of the future, or depressed at your financial situation, your body may well interpret these messages from the mind as life-threatening and will increase the stress response in preparation for fight-or-flight. The reverse is also true: by changing your thoughts to positive ones you can begin to transform and improve your well-being.

visions of peace Just for a moment, close your eyes and visualize yourself running and see if this causes your muscles to tense. Imagine you are eating a slice of lemon, and feel the saliva increase in your mouth. Now picture yourself standing beside a beautiful waterfall cascading down among large rocks. A cool spray is falling on your face, the smell of the cold water is in your nose, and you can feel your body releasing and letting go. Stay with this image for a few minutes and then see how you feel. Relaxed?

Imagining a beautiful or peaceful scene triggers the relaxation response, while increasing feelings of tranquillity, love, inner strength and courage. It replenishes our emotional stores and eases inner tension. To use visualization for stress release, it is important to select images that are simple, free of detail, soothing and that feel safe – images of floating in gentle waves as they lap close to the shore, or of lying in a field of wild flowers, are ideal for overworked brains. If the imagery is too complicated it will engage too much mental energy; the relaxation will be deeper the more we are able to let go of any distractions. Practise this

whenever you need to – at the office, on a crowded train, when sitting quietly. Simply let your mind rest in that place of ease and beauty.

Just as you can create a relaxing picture inside your mind, so you can imagine yourself in everyday life, whether at work responding to instructions, being relaxed at meetings, or being creative with the demands of friends or family. Visualize an image of yourself as you would like to be for at least five minutes before the event. Then watch what happens.

We can also use visualization to ask our inner self for guidance and help by imagining a meeting with a wise being. This personal mentor represents all the knowledge that we already have within us. The visualization merely enables us to tap into this wisdom and bring it into the conscious mind. Take your time to relax and develop a peaceful image, such as walking through a wood or beside a tranquil lake, before you visualize meeting your guide, moving more deeply into the unconscious. You can share anything you want with your guide, then be responsive to hearing their words. Do not judge, but receive with an open heart.

supportive steps in the seven step programme
Visualizations are included in the relaxation practices in each step, and you can create your own at any time.

creative visualization

To create a visualization, find a comfortable place to sit or lie down, then breathe and relax for a few minutes before you start.

Begin by creating in your mind's eye a perfect but imaginary place in nature. Put into it all the natural features that you find beautiful and peaceful. See the colours, hear the sounds, feel the sun, the ground, explore the landscape. Are there birds or animals here? Are there forests, mountains or water? This is your special place, known only to you, somewhere you know you belong and are safe.

In this place you can forget all your concerns, all your fears, all the details of your life – you can just be yourself. Nothing else is going on. Just let yourself be here, basking in the quiet and the peace. Sometimes you may meet another being in your visualization, perhaps an animal, a bird, or even a person. These represent aspects of your inner wisdom, so if they come spontaneously, ask them for guidance or healing.

You can come back to this, your special place, whenever you choose – it is always with you.

the practice of
meditation

Do you ever have moments when you are so completely absorbed that you forget yourself? Many of us experience such a moment spontaneously, perhaps when sitting quietly in the open air or engrossed in a creative project. Suddenly, the boundaries that normally isolate us evaporate and we are at one with the clouds, the birds, the river, the trees. This is an experience of meditation, where we enter a deep, quiet space within, going beyond our individual concerns, fears and needs. It brings us a sense of relief, of coming home, of a place we have always yearned for without knowing where or what it was. It is a place of profound peace.

However, the mind is constantly jumping from one thought to the next, forever distracted and preoccupied. So for the mind to do our bidding – for it to find that quiet space within – takes more than just sitting beside a river. We practise meditation in order to consciously quieten the mind, to release the chatter and to bring it to a simple, clear and peaceful place. The technique is a way of giving the mind something to do, and is a tool for focusing and for developing specific states of being. In this way, the mind will slowly calm down, the thoughts becoming less frequent. Meditation takes place in the space between the thoughts and induces a complete relaxation of our whole being. During meditation we have the chance to see how our minds work – how the dramas come and go or how we get lost in anxieties – and to discover greater self-awareness, self-acceptance and self-knowledge.

There are many forms of meditation practice and no single way is more effective than another – one teacher told us that there are as many techniques as there are people who practise them. We each develop our own style to fit our needs. In other words, there is no right or wrong way, no special secret method; often, the simpler the technique the more effective it will be. The techniques used in this book have been used for thousands of years throughout the many spiritual traditions of the world.

six mini-meditations Each step of the programme offers specific relaxation and meditation exercises, but we do not have to limit ourselves to this formal practice time. We can practise meditation anywhere we are, even if it is only for a few moments. For instance, right now, as you read this, just stop and take three breaths. Focusing on the out breath, count one as you breathe out, then two on the next out breath, then three on the next. Just three breaths. Feel the difference? A mini-meditation like this brings us back to our centre, reminding us of our peace. It harmonizes the body and balances our energies. We live in a crowded and demanding world so it is vital that we find space and quiet within ourselves. Listed below are six mini-meditations you can practise in between various other activities, perhaps when your family is involved in other things, in your lunch hour at work, or even as you walk down the street.

instant inner conscious relaxation
Either sit in an upright chair or lie on the floor, somewhere where you will not be disturbed. Start by watching the breath as it enters and leaves your body.

the path of awareness

Breathe out tension, breathe in ease for a count of three breaths. Then relax your body by silently naming and visualizing each part. Start with the right hand ... arm ... down the right side of the body ... the leg ... ankle and foot ... then the left hand ... arm ... left side of the body ... leg ... ankle and foot ... then the buttocks ... all the way up the back ... the right and left shoulders ... then the genitals ... abdomen ... chest ... neck ... and the whole of your head. Take a few deep breaths and gently stretch your whole body.

instant visualization Find a quiet place to lie or sit. Spend a few moments breathing and relaxing your whole body. Then imagine you are lying on a soft, sandy beach. The water is blue and calm, palm trees line the shore. Imagine that your breaths are like the waves of the ocean. With each in breath the water is washing over your body, with each out breath it is taking away any tension, stress, anxiety ... feel it all being released. If you like, enter the water and swim or float, weightless and free, letting the water support you. Feel the sun warming your body. Stay here for a few minutes, flowing with your breath and the gentle rhythm of the waves. When you feel ready, gently come back to sit on the shore for a few moments before the visualization fades.

instant breath meditation Sit comfortably with your back straight. Take a deep breath and let it go. Breathing normally, begin to count silently at the end of each out breath. Inhale ... exhale ... count one, inhale ... exhale ... two, inhale ... exhale ...

three. Then start at one again. Just three breaths. Now follow each breath in, counting silently, one, two, three. So simple. Do this as many times as you want, keeping your eyes open or closed, whatever feels right for you.

instant walking meditation You can do this along a country lane, a city street, in the office or in the garden. You can walk slowly, normally or fast – whatever feels right for you. Start walking and, as you walk, become aware of the movement of your body and the rise and fall of your feet. Become aware of your breath and see if you can stay in touch with both your breathing and your walking at the same time. Walk and breathe with awareness for a few minutes.

instant deep breathing Find a quiet place to be alone. Sit with a straight back and relax. Begin by focusing on the in and out rhythm of your breath until it settles naturally. Then take a deep breath and fill the belly, the middle chest and the upper chest, then empty the upper chest, middle chest and belly. Do this slowly five times and, as you breathe, visualize all the tension in your body being released on each out breath.

instant letting go Find a quiet place to sit, have a straight back, and take a deep breath and let it go. Then quietly repeat to yourself, 'My body is released and relaxed ... my heartbeat is normal ... my mind is calm and peaceful ... my heart is open and loving.' Keep repeating this until you have let go of any tension and you feel completely at ease. Then take a deep breath and have a smile on your face!

supportive steps in the seven step programme

There are two types of meditation technique: those that develop greater states of concentration and clarity of mind; and those that develop specific states of being that transcend our normal ego-centred states. We have included both types in the programme.

we are **what we eat**

The food we eat has a direct effect on our physical, mental and emotional health. They are all dependent on the right proportion of nutrients – what we eat today we walk and talk tomorrow! An inadequate diet strains the digestive system, over-stimulates the nervous system and puts excess pressure on the heart, all known stressors. Poor nutrition can lead to exhaustion, susceptibility to colds and infections, skin disorders, digestive problems and headaches.

With today's busy lifestyle, we have little time available to be selective when buying food, or to cook dishes that need a long preparation. Our preference is to buy ready-made foods such as tinned vegetables and fruit, sliced and packaged bread, frozen pizzas or chips, sauces that come out of a jar, biscuits and sweetened cereals. We trust that the instant, processed foods we buy are not only edible, but also provide us with adequate nutrition.

This is not always the case. Tinned foods are invariably overcooked, and pre-prepared vegetables lose much of their goodness after being peeled and exposed to air. All refined products (white bread, pasta or rice) are missing the essential balance of components they had as whole grains, leaving them with little to offer but carbohydrate. In their unrefined form (such as wholewheat bread and brown rice) we gain vitamin E, protein and excellent roughage.

The picture is not much better when we come to many of the so-called fresh foods we buy at the supermarket. We are told, for example, that fresh fruit and vegetables are the best source for essential vitamins and minerals, but once they have been picked, packaged and transported to the shops, that nutritional level begins to fall. A few days under the bright lights at a supermarket and there will be little vitamin content left. Modern farming methods also result in nutrient deficiency and rely heavily on potentially harmful chemical fertilizers and pesticides.

Excess sugar, present in many instant foods and in soft and fizzy drinks, leads to hyperactivity, depression, irritability and exhaustion. Too much fat (from fatty meats, dairy produce and fried foods) strains the liver, causing headaches, indigestion, sluggishness and lethargy. Drinking too many cups of tea and coffee can result in palpitations, nervousness, irritability and exhaustion, as well as headaches.

eating well Now the good news. It *is* possible to change your diet to one that supports a strong, healthy and energetic lifestyle. It may take a while to establish new patterns of eating, but once you do you should feel the difference very quickly. Your aim is to balance the nervous system, build the body's defences against infection, and strengthen your physical resources, giving you more energy, both physically and mentally. We suggest that you drink plenty of water each day (most experts agree on three pints a day being about right). Eat fresh fruit at any time, especially in the morning, and make sure that vegetables make up the bulk of at least one if not two meals. Through these foods you gain the vitamins and minerals you need, roughage to keep the intestines working, and enzymes to stimulate digestion. But they must be as fresh as possible and, ideally, grown using organic methods. And don't overcook your vegetables in lots of boiling water, or most of the goodness will end up going down the drain with the cooking water. Instead, try quick stir-frying, baking, steaming, or eating them raw in salads.

Keep dairy foods to a minimum, especially full-fat products. They can safely be replaced with skimmed milk and low-fat cheeses – these have less fat but plenty of protein and calcium – or with soya milk products. Tofu, which is also made from soya beans, is an easily digested form of vegetable protein. Protein can also be obtained from nuts, sesame seeds, sunflower seeds, pulses, fish and lean meats. All wheat or rice products should be whole grain. You might also like to try other grains, such as millet, barley or buckwheat. Try substituting muesli or porridge for sweet breakfast cereals, and replacing heavy desserts with dried fruits, such as dates or apricots, or with fresh fruits and soya yogurt. Experiment with caffeine alternatives such as grain coffees and herb teas. Drink real fruit juices instead of alcohol. And watch your energy levels rise!

supportive steps in the seven step programme

Throughout the programme, we will make dietary suggestions to increase your overall well-being. Occasional fasting and eating only certain foods help purify the body as part of the healing process. You can work with these suggestions to find what is best for you.

moving and shaking

The mind and body are so interconnected that we really cannot think of them as two separate things – one is constantly affecting the other. When we are angry, our movements become strong and expansive; when we are sad, they become weak and withdrawn. Where relaxation and meditation are vital for bringing balance to the mind and for calming our physiological reactions to stress, movement and exercise are necessary for releasing the physical effects of stress from the body.

The benefits of exercise are enormous. Most importantly, exercise enables any repressed frustration, anxiety and fear to leave the body. The more we are absorbed in the physical process, the less attention we pay to what is going on in the mind, which eases layers of deeper tension. Exercise also encourages the release of hormones, such as endorphins, that stimulate feelings of well-being and happiness; this is what is known as 'runner's high'.

When we are stressed, we often hold back or resist our feelings, which can manifest physically in stiff muscles, aching or tiredness. Exercise helps to release this stiffness and enables us to have greater physical expression. Experiments carried out in homes for the elderly have found that within only a few weeks of gentle exercise and weight lifting, residents were regaining flexibility and mobility, muscles were rebuilding and joints loosening; the participants were also considerably happier, more animated and talkative. As we move the body, so we move the mind and open the heart, gaining greater mental and emotional flexibility and freedom. Exercise and movement also enable us to feel better about ourselves: with a stronger, more energized body comes greater self-esteem and confidence. Sleep tends to be deeper and we awaken more rested; headaches or stress-related physical problems are lessened; concentration and alertness are increased.

get exercising Exercising does not mean that you have to go against your body's natural inclinations. Some people are built to be joggers, while others are born walkers or dancers. It is vital that you find a form of movement that you enjoy and that can be integrated into your day. If jogging or walking is your favourite way to get moving, then develop a route and a time of day to which you can commit yourself. Without that commitment, the time will come and go, filled with other things that need to be done.

walking Brisk walking is a very important form of movement as it stimulates the circulation and the nervous system, while loosening and relaxing the

the path of awareness

entire body. If you have never exercised before, start with just a ten-minute walk or gentle jog every day for a week, then make it 15 minutes every day. Do a little more each week. After a week or two, try adding a different form of exercise to your regular one – do some yoga stretches (see below), or go swimming – so that you use other muscles.

dance There is nothing more wonderfully, emotionally expressive than dance. Make a time when you can be alone and play your favourite dance music as loud as you can – then get moving! Open your body and move freely, dancing and singing your stress and anxieties into a joyful sequence of bends, lifts and spins. Or take a friend and go out dancing together so that you can encourage each other.

yoga This ancient physical discipline moves every part of the body into new and wondrous places, invigorating and rebalancing the nerves, opening the joints, helping the spine become more supple, and releasing any tension or tightness; it also has a very healing and calming effect on the mind. The movements are performed with awareness of the breath and body together. Look out for a class that is taught locally – apart from the benefits of having a teacher, it is fun to do yoga with others.

martial arts Chi Kung and Tai Chi are particularly well-known martial arts, and both are wonderful for releasing stress and building inner strength. The Chinese consider Tai Chi to be so valuable that its practice is recommended for many physical and psychological ailments, as well as for the prevention of disease. You can see it practised every morning in city parks in Chinese communities all over the world. Joining a class is the best way for beginners to start to learn these movement systems.

supportive steps in the seven step programme

Many of the exercises in the programme are based on yoga postures, so you will be introduced to the benefits of the discipline. **Steps 4** and **5** invite you to dance in a way that you never have before. Walking is often suggested as a warm-up to exercise.

the seven step programme

introducing the
programme
The Seven Step Programme offers a comprehensive training in relaxation and meditation. It allows the beginner to both understand and practise these techniques, and the more experienced practitioner to deepen their experience of them. Each step builds on the one before it, ensuring that the programme has flow and continuity. It is recommended that you spend a minimum of one week on each step, but you can take longer if you want to, anything up to a few months per step. Or you may like to go through the whole programme – taking seven weeks to do it – and then go back to those parts of the programme that you found most beneficial and develop these further. Remember, it takes time to overcome doubt or boredom, for the mind to quieten and for you to feel at ease within yourself. The eventual aim of the programme is for you to go beyond the seven steps outlined in this book and evolve your own approach to relaxation and meditation.

Each step of the programme has its own theme, progressing through what are known as the seven chakras (see pages 68–69). The steps include both a morning and an evening routine, which consist of movement and relaxation or meditation, together with suggestions for lifestyle changes to complement the exercises, and affirmations and inspirational thoughts around the theme. Nothing is compulsory: do only what feels right for you, and only to the best of your ability. You are not doing this to create more stress or pain!

To begin with you will need to spend about 30 minutes in the morning and evening on the programme – around one hour per day. You can increase the amount of time you spend each day as you feel ready or have more time available. It may mean making changes in your schedule, perhaps getting up earlier, arranging for extra childcare, watching less television, or allocating jobs to other people. So much of our time is spent on entertainment or on things that are less important than our well-being. You don't have to clean the house twice a week or make breakfast for everyone – they can do it themselves. Rather than putting time for yourself last on the list of things to be done, put yourself first for these seven weeks and then see how you feel. This time for you is precious, so do respect it.

You are now ready to embark on the programme. Congratulations, you are beginning a wondrous and joyful journey!

how to practise

Creating the right environment in which to practise relaxation or meditation can make quite a difference to our ability to focus. Ideally, we have a room for each of our daily activities – a bedroom for sleeping, a kitchen for cooking and eating, a study for working – which is most conducive to that activity. The same applies to meditation and relaxation. On the one hand, we can, of course, practise anywhere – all we need is to sit or lie down and close our eyes. And yet creating a space at home which we use just for this activity creates a feeling of specialness, of reverence and self-respect. Given that prayer and worship are the main activities that take place in a church, it is not surprising that such buildings often have a profoundly spiritual feel. In the same way, when we create a particular space in which to practise relaxation and meditation, it develops its own potency.

Find a space where you can be quiet, undisturbed and warm. When you do the Seven Step Programme you will be coming here twice a day, so make it a place that expresses your commitment to your well-being. You can put a small table there for flowers, a candle, or any other objects that feel precious to you. If you do not have a separate space that you can use, then find a particular part of a room where you feel most at ease and always use the same spot.

Find a time that works for you both morning and evening. Work within the time frame of your own needs. Some people prefer to read the relaxation and meditation exercises on to a cassette so that they do not have to memorize the instructions, or to read them at the same time as doing the practice. (Cassettes are also available from the authors, details on page 159.)

When you practise Inner Conscious Relaxation in the Seven Step Programme, you will be lying on the floor, so have a blanket or rug to lie on. When you practise meditation, you will be sitting, either on cushions on the floor or on a chair (see pages 62–63). In the relaxation or meditation process, your body temperature can drop, so have a light blanket or shawl over you to keep you warm. However, you don't want to be too warm or you will soon fall asleep! Always wear loose clothing, something that feels comfortable, as it is important that the body can move freely without restrictions. Remove your glasses or watch, undo your belt – this all helps the body to relax.

Remember to turn off the telephone, and if you think your family or housemates might disturb you, put a note on the door letting them know what time you will be finished. It is important that your family do not resent you having this time to yourself, so tell them how much you need to de-stress, and how it will make you a much nicer person to live with. Share with them what is involved so that they do not feel excluded or concerned. If you try eating in a different way, using any of the dietary suggestions made, or exercising more, then include your family so that they see how they could also make changes, even if they are not yet ready to do so. Do not force your programme on them – let them change when they are ready.

the right posture

Having the correct posture for relaxation and meditation will make an enormous difference to your practice – one meditation teacher has even said that posture *is* meditation. So taking the time to get this right is very important.

For relaxation the correct position is lying on your back on a blanket or mat on the floor (**figure ❶**). Do not use a bed, unless you need to, or you may find that you soon fall asleep. Have a light blanket to cover you and a small pillow for your head. Arms are by your sides, palms facing upwards, legs are slightly apart, eyes are closed. If lying down is difficult, relaxation can be done in an upright chair, with feet flat on the ground, hands on the lap with palms facing upwards.

The most important element of the meditation posture is a straight back, which means that you must be sitting upright, unless you physically need to lie down.

The reasons why a straight back is so important are, first, it keeps you awake and alert. Second, when the back is upright, it is in its natural position and it hardly has to do any work in order to maintain that position, so it will not ache so readily; a bent back has to work the muscles to stay bent and will soon cause discomfort. And third, a straight back makes it easier to breathe freely, while a rounded back constricts the breathing. This is especially important for meditations that focus on the breath. When the posture is wrong, it will cause aching muscles and discomfort; when it is right, it creates an inner stillness that promotes a deeply meditative state.

There are a variety of postures which can help maintain a straight back. The traditional posture for meditation is sitting cross-legged on the floor, with one or two cushions beneath your buttocks. When the base of the spine is lifted higher than the knees in this way, the blood flows more

⑤

easily; too low, and the back will curve and you will get pins and needles in your legs. There are a number of positions outlined below, all of which work well. Vary the number of cushions or the type of chair you need until you find the posture that feels most comfortable. Use firm cushions (such as those filled with kapok or foam), as they will support you better than soft ones. If you do sit on the floor, also have a folded blanket or foam mat under you to pad your knees and ankles.

The simplest position is the ordinary cross-legged posture in **figure ②**. Note that this position usually requires more cushions to lift the spine higher than the knees. In **figure ③** the legs are further apart and the knees touch the ground, one leg in front of the other. This is a very popular posture, as it puts little strain on the legs and it lifts the spine. Again, experiment with the cushions, as you may find using more is better. In **figure ④** one foot is resting on the other leg. This is wonderful for the spine, as it provides a firm support and uprightness, but be careful not to strain your knees if you are not used to sitting like this.

In many countries a small wooden stool is used instead of cushions, as shown in **figure ⑤**. Here you kneel with your legs under the stool. Make sure that you have a thick blanket or pad beneath your legs to cushion your shins and ankles. You can also sit with cushions between your buttocks and your calves to create the same posture. This position puts no strain on the legs while easily lifting the spine, as the stool slopes slightly forwards. A different type of stool is the kneeling chair seen in **figure ⑥**. This is found in many office or furniture shops and is very comfortable for meditation, especially as you can adjust the height to suit your needs. There is no strain on any part of the body; the whole purpose of the chair is to lift the spine upright.

⑥

Alternatively, you can use a straight-backed chair, as shown in **figure ⑦**. Do not use a soft armchair, as this will round your back, making it harder to breathe freely. A little cushion in the small of your back can help to support your spine. Have your feet flat on the floor so that the body is not restricted in any way.

When sitting for meditation, your shoulders should be relaxed and sloping slightly backwards. Hands should be folded in your lap or resting on your thighs, facing either up or down. The head is straight. Eyes are gently closed, unless you have a tendency to nod off to sleep, in which case you should have them slightly open but looking softly at the ground a little way in front of you.

⑦

taming the monkey mind

When you first begin to practise relaxation and meditation you will probably be amazed at how much noise there is in your head: the endless thinking, the dramas and scenarios, anxieties, conversations and images that seem never-ending – we go from thought to thought like a monkey leaping from branch to branch. What we do not realize is that this goes on all the time, but we are rarely quiet enough to notice. In the process of seeking that still place inside you for the first time, you will get to see everything there is between you and the stillness.

It is absolutely normal to be distracted during meditation – it was once estimated that most people have distracting thoughts up to 200 to 300 times per half hour! Knowing this can help you accept your own experiences more easily. You are not alone in having a constant stream of thoughts, or, for that matter, a body that keeps coming up with different aches and pains. Do not think that this means you cannot meditate. No one can fully quieten the mind – that would be like trying to catch the wind – but what we can do is learn to stop resisting it.

During the practice of relaxation or meditation, every time you notice you have drifted off into your thoughts, silently repeat, 'Thinking, thinking, thinking', and then come back to the practice. Or see your thoughts as birds in the sky and watch them fly away. Become the observer of your thinking rather than be immersed in the thoughts. It does not matter what the thoughts are, just observe them and let them go. All sorts of issues will arise to grab your attention, but just keep coming back to yourself. Think of your mind as a monkey you are slowly taming. By becoming aware of how the mind operates, you will find you are less distracted by it, less subject to every whim.

As you persevere, you will get glimpses of that quiet and still place. These glimpses will grow. This is important, as it is so easy to judge – whether it is judging ourselves, our thoughts, our progress or seeming lack of it, other people, or even the technique itself as wrong or useless. Simply label this 'Judging, judging, judging', and let it go. Or try counting your judgements – by the time you get to judgement number 300 you will be laughing at yourself! All this helps you to grow in patience and compassion for yourself. Know that each one of us has to deal with the monkey mind. It is like looking in a dusty mirror – the thoughts and distractions are the dust but, beneath that, the glass is clear.

During your practice you may find important issues arising that do need to have time given to thinking them through. Rather than doing this during your practice time, make a mental note of the issue and promise yourself to come back to it when you have finished your session. If you do this, then it will be easier to let go of the issue and to continue without further distraction.

beating the boredom Boredom is another issue that often arises when practising relaxation and meditation, particularly if you are used to having a very active mind. It can seem like madness to be spending a whole half hour just sitting still and watching your breath. Soon you become bored and restless, wanting to get up and do something else. However, the repetitive nature of the practice is very purposeful; it is there to enable you to go beyond the doubt and confusion, boredom and lethargy. Keep at it and the practice will eventually pull you deeper and deeper into yourself and you will then see why you are doing it.

Your ability to relax may be erratic. You may find you have a wonderfully peaceful session one day and think you are really getting somewhere, only to have a boring or noisy session the next day, where you do nothing but drift off into fantasy land. This is normal. Do not judge yourself as hopeless – judgement is just another way the ego tries to distract you from the practice. You are simply gaining insight into the nature of the mind. Instead, watch how all things come and go, appear and disappear, how nothing stays the same.

suspending judgement Learning to tame the monkey mind comes back to accepting ourselves. As long as we resist or judge our discursive thoughts, restless mind, hopeless posture or inability to stay still, we are not accepting ourselves as we are.

One of the purposes of the practice is for us to see ourselves more clearly, but we must combine this with a deeper acceptance, rather than being ashamed or having a sense of hopelessness at what we find. If we can accept whatever our mind comes up with as just another aspect of the mind, but not as something to be taken seriously, then soon the mind will not trouble you so much.

Many people think they must be bad practitioners or that these techniques are not for them, simply because their minds are filled with different thoughts or images, or they get uncomfortable or restless. Nobody has told them that this is normal! It does take time to train both the mind and the body – so perseverance is essential. There is no such thing as a good or bad practitioner. We are all capable of connecting with the stillness inside ourselves, it just may not happen all at once. That is why we have suggested you take as much time as you need with each step of the programme.

Be patient, be gentle. You are a practitioner, not a master. Your practice is there to be your friend not your enemy, so make it enjoyable and fun, something you want to do.

daily activities

How we integrate the programme into our lives will be different for each one of us, but the best way to help yourself is to make it a part of your whole life, not just something you do for half an hour here and there.

The commitment to your overall well-being is vital — the more you truly see the need for change, and the greater your desire for deeper happiness and more meaning in your life, the more this will carry you through any doubts or lapses. To some extent, you must trust the process — not everything will improve immediately — but as you progress with the programme, so your relationships, your enjoyment of life, your health, your loving and caring, your creativity, energy, confidence and capabilities will become increasingly uplifted and renewed. Allow your commitment, and your responsibility to yourself, to permeate your day, influencing your interactions with others and your desire to exercise, eat well, play more and be kinder to yourself. Remember that you are not doing this to impress or please someone else — this is something that you are doing for yourself.

As you begin the programme, start to note your feelings as you progress through each day, observing how they change from week to week. Let each moment be one of transformation. For instance, become aware of how you normally feel when you first wake up in the morning. Make a note of your earliest thoughts or sensations, how your body feels and what your energy level is like. Do you wake up groggy and stiff, dreading the day ahead, wishing you could disappear under the bedclothes? Do you awaken gently, reaching out into the world to see what is there, breathing in the new day? Or do you instantly leap out of bed, all systems go, ready to put as much into the day as you possibly can?

If you feel that your start to the day needs improving, pay more attention to your first waking moments. As you feel yourself stirring, use these few minutes to set the tone for your whole day by creating positive, loving, trusting and welcoming thoughts (see opposite).

Extend your awareness to each moment of your day. When you get up, do you normally head for the coffee or tea straight away? Do you automatically put the toast on or are you always so late that you have to rush out of the house without time to feed yourself? Try using these early moments of your day to honour yourself, to breathe in and out with awareness, to nourish and nurture your mind and body. Make your first drink one that is welcomed by your body, perhaps some hot water with honey and lemon (absolutely delicious and refreshing!) or a soothing herb tea. Make sure that you have time to eat some breakfast calmly and with attention, and that you take in food that reflects your care for yourself — perhaps some fruit, yogurt or muesli.

As the day progresses, watch where you start speeding up and moving into automatic ways of thinking and behaving. At which points in your day do you switch into high gear and forget about your breathing? When do you reach for the coffee and forget about equanimity? What makes you impatient so that you forget about spaciousness and generosity? Pay attention to the messages your body sends you and how your thoughts and feelings might be affecting you physically.

Throughout this day I am loving and considerate of both myself and others.

I welcome this new day as a day of unlimited potential and beauty.

(MORNING THOUGHTS) This day is completely new. It is filled with joy

and creativity.

Today I am completely spontaneous and imaginative.

I receive this day as a precious gift to be treasured and enjoyed.

I give thanks for the beauty that was in this day, that it may continue to

(EVENING THOUGHTS) nourish me as I sleep.

This day was perfect in itself, offering me the lessons I most need to learn.

I let this day rest with joy and gratitude, and thank my body for its

work that it may now rest.

As the day moves into evening, be aware of your behaviour and needs. Do you automatically get yourself a drink? Or do you fall asleep while watching television? Are you unable to wind down and let the day go without some form of distraction? Try a soothing drink like chamomile tea and honey instead of alcohol; listen to classical music or go for a walk instead of vegetating in front of the television. Then do your evening practice and let your day come to a gentle conclusion.

At the end of the day take a few moments before you go to sleep to reconnect with yourself, examining your thoughts and feelings about the day that has passed. Reflect on the gifts and opportunities that you have received and turn your thoughts to ones of gratitude and completion as you release any difficulties that may have arisen (see above). See if you can transform any problems you encountered that day into blessings.

the chakras

The Seven Step Programme progresses through the seven chakras. According to ancient Indian belief, these are major energy centres which are accessed through specific points on the spinal column and which influence our perception of reality. Each one represents a different level of awakening – from instinctive, self-centred behaviour to higher states of compassion and wisdom. So as we proceed through the programme we deepen our awareness of and sensitivity to both ourselves and others, moving from the mundane to the profound.

root chakra This first chakra is located at the perineum in men, the cervix in women. It represents our most basic instincts for survival and self-protection, and is associated with the colour red. The root chakra also relates to our ancestral history and to our sense of belonging, of having a valid place in the world. If the energy here is inactive, then we cower in the face of difficulties, and we may feel that we are not safe or supported. When this chakra is awakened, we meet challenges with optimism and creativity, we have trust in the world and a loving acceptance of ourselves.

base chakra The second chakra is located at the base of the spine and is associated with the colour orange. The base chakra represents the area of relationship, which encompasses intimacy, communication, sharing and parenting, as well as the realm of pleasure. It corresponds to the conditioned mind and the habits that control our behaviour. With an unawakened base chakra, desire can lead to greed, a longing for more and a general feeling of dissatisfaction. An awakened base chakra leads to a greater ease in relating to others, an ability to balance our own needs with those of others, and an acceptance of ourselves as being an interconnected part of a greater whole.

solar plexus chakra The third chakra is situated in the spine behind the navel and its colour is yellow. It is associated with the beginning of the individuation process, i.e. the development of the ego into a separate self which possesses personal power. Unawakened, the third chakra gives rise to a false sense of power and a need to control others. It can also manifest itself as a fear of responsibility – we have to be told what to do rather than taking the initiative. This chakra gives great meaning and direction to life – the process of becoming an individual is one of finding our own inner authority. An awakened third chakra ensures a healthy, positive and confident sense of self.

heart chakra The fourth chakra is located in the spine directly behind the centre of the chest, and is associated with a rose pink colour. This chakra enables us to evolve into a truly loving person by opening the heart to altruism, compassion and a feeling that we are intimately connected to all other beings. An unawakened heart chakra is seen in a closed or cold heart, in someone who is unable to care either for him- or herself or anyone else. There may be feelings of being unlovable, a fear of loving, jealousy or deep sorrow. An open heart chakra is an infinite source of love and compassion – the more the heart opens, the more love fills our being.

throat chakra The fifth chakra is allied to the throat in the spinal region and is represented by the colour turquoise. This chakra is the gateway to our whole being, where we both take in nourishment and share our feelings outwardly. When the throat chakra is not awakened, we may feel that we have no voice, or that we are out of touch with our deeper feelings. When the throat chakra is activated, it leads to a deep healing of our inner being, and a transformation of our negative perceptions into positive ones.

third eye chakra The sixth chakra is located in the space behind the centre of the eyebrows. Symbolized as a third eye and by a violet colour, this chakra is the eye of wisdom that looks from within and sees the truth. It is identified with the mind and higher consciousness, and in particular with the development of perception and intuition. Through the third eye we can penetrate the nature of reality and discover the truth within ourselves.

crown chakra The seventh chakra is located at the top of the head and is represented by all the colours of the rainbow. This chakra is seen as the penultimate human experience, the opening into spiritual and cosmic consciousness. Here our personal desires are purified and our actions become selfless and joyful. We find our deepest place of equanimity, an unshakable core that is always at peace.

introducing the programme

69

finding our
rightful place

The programme begins by focusing on our relationship to ourselves. In particular, Step I emphasizes the importance of discovering our place in the world, and of being confident in our right to be here. It is essential to start with self-acceptance, as everything we do, everything we feel, all our beliefs, attitudes and thoughts stem from our sense of being and belonging. If we feel unsure of ourselves or uneasy in our world, then we are like a small frightened bird that flits from one branch to another, startled by the slightest sound. When we are inwardly calm and relaxed, we are less easily disturbed and more content with our world. This relates to the first chakra and our sense of safety and security.

Stress isolates us, loneliness isolates us, feeling we are not being heard, recognized or loved isolates us. When stress becomes distress we tend to push other people away. Because we believe our feelings are too painful to bear, we try to bury them; in the process, we may become so cut off that we are unsympathetic and uncaring towards others.

One who is anciently aware of existence,
Is master of every moment,
Feels no break since time beyond time
In the way life flows. LAO TZU

We do not believe that we belong, that we are all connected in some way. We think that we can hurt someone else and not be hurt ourselves. We do not see that our pain is also the pain of others. We do not feel any responsibility towards the trees or the oceans, towards our world or to the beings in it.

While it is true that we are each unique, separate individuals, at the same time we are not alone – we are all interconnected, walking the same earth and breathing the same air. All things, all life is interrelated. To understand this better for yourself, see if you can find the place where you start, the point at which, before you existed, there was nothing. Or the point at which your food came into being. Or the source of water. Can you find one? Or do you keep going from one connection to the next, from your body to those of your parents and then your grandparents, or from the loaf of bread to the baker, to the wheat, to the grain, to the rain and the sun and the earth? Viewing all life from this perspective, can we say that we are separate from the food we eat or the water we drink? Is there anything that is independent, unconnected or truly alone?

No matter how difficult the past, you can always begin again today. THE BUDDHA

I am a child of the universe, the world is my home, all beings are my family.

When we really feel our interconnectedness, we realize that even our thoughts, let alone our actions, have an impact, and that we are all co-creators of our world; then all life becomes precious and meaningful. Rather than seeing ourselves or our family as the centre of our universe, we see that we are a part of a beautiful, profoundly mysterious, interconnecting, intercommunicating dynamic, where nothing is more important than anything else and no one is greater or lesser. We are all here together, with and for each other.

Spend this first step of the programme being aware of your connectedness to all people and to the world around you. Explore your family history; focus on your relatives and the ancestral lineage that gives you a sense of belonging, of your place in the world. Go back even further to your lost ancestors. Also recall past friends or teachers who have been there for you, and think of the tribe of friends or family you are now connected with, and how each one adds something different to your life. Recognize your moments of insecurity and fear, your times of doubt and confusion, and remind yourself that you are important, that you are safe, that you do belong, and that you are loved.

One's distance from heaven is in proportion to the measure of one's self-love. EMANUEL SWEDENBORG

stretching (15–20 minutes)

standing pose *This is a simple posture which aligns your whole body.* Stand with your feet just a few inches apart and face forwards, your arms by your side, and your eyes looking ahead or closed. Very gently begin to straighten, as if a string is slowly pulling you upwards from a central point at the very top of your head. As you lift upwards, let your abdomen come in and your shoulders drop back.

Slowly feel your spine lifting up, your chest opening and your neck lengthening. Now feel your whole spine lengthening, as if there is space between each vertebra. Remember to keep breathing – this is not a tense pose, just a natural opening of the body. Feel this elongation from the soles of your feet to the top of your head. Stay like this for a few minutes.

Now, very slowly, begin to feel the string unwinding. Let your body come to a normal upright position, with your back straight. Feel the dignity and inner strength in your uprightness. Take a deep breath.

These simple exercises release any tension in the joints, loosening the whole body. Only do as much as you can.

head roll Staying in a standing position, gently and slowly rotate your head, letting it fall forwards, sideways, back and sideways the other way as best you can. Do this three times in each direction. When you have finished, stand for a moment and take a deep breath.

shoulder lift Still standing, and keeping your arms down, lift your shoulders as high as you can ... keep lifting ... keep lifting ... and then let them drop back. Take a deep breath.

You can stand or sit upright for the following exercises.

finger stretch Hold your arms out in front of you and stretch out the fingers of both hands, then close them into fists. Repeat five times.

wrist stretch Flex your wrists with the fingers pointing up, as if you are pressing your hands against a wall, then flex and point downwards. Repeat five times.

wrist turn Form a loose fist and rotate the wrists, five times clockwise and five times anticlockwise.

elbow stretch Stretch both arms out to the sides, then bend the arms so that your hands touch your shoulders, then stretch out again. Make sure this movement is slow and precise, not jerky. Repeat five times.

shoulder rotation Place your hands on your shoulders and rotate your shoulders five times forwards and five times backwards, as if drawing circles with your elbows (see left). Make the movement as large as possible, bringing the elbows together where they naturally meet at chest level.

arm stretch Lift the left arm up, reaching above your head as far as possible, stretching the left side. Then lower and repeat on the right side.

You will need to sit on the floor for the following exercises.

toe stretch Stretch both legs out in front of you, supporting yourself by placing your hands on the floor slightly behind you. Stretch your toes out and clench them back five times.

ankle stretch Flex the ankles by stretching the feet forwards and then backwards, really pointing your toes. Do this five times, working the instep.

ankle turn Move the legs slightly apart and slowly rotate the ankles, five times clockwise and five times anticlockwise.

knee bend

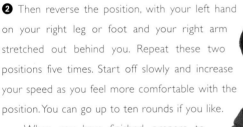

1 Bend the right leg at the knee and support it under the thigh with your hands, your foot flexed backwards with the toes pointing up.

2 Bring the thigh as close to your chest as you can, keeping your back straight, then straighten the leg out without your foot touching the ground, toes pointing forwards. Do this five times, then repeat with the left leg five times.

spinal turn

1 Spread your legs a foot or so apart. Keep your arms straight and take your right hand to your left leg, as far as you can reach, while looking over your left shoulder and stretching your left arm out behind you. Try to keep your back as straight as possible without rounding your shoulders.

2 Then reverse the position, with your left hand on your right leg or foot and your right arm stretched out behind you. Repeat these two positions five times. Start off slowly and increase your speed as you feel more comfortable with the position. You can go up to ten rounds if you like.

When you have finished, prepare to practise Inner Conscious Relaxation.

inner **conscious relaxation** (15 minutes)

Find a comfortable position, lying down on a mat or blanket and using a small pillow, as instructed on page 62. Remember to wear loose, comfortable clothing, have a light blanket to cover you, and ensure that you will not be disturbed. Have your arms by your sides, palms facing upwards, and your legs slightly apart. Relax your head and close your eyes. Take a deep breath and blow it out.

Relax your body by bringing awareness to your toes and working your way up the body, releasing tension wherever it may appear ... ankles ... calves ... knees ... thighs ... buttocks ... back of the body ... pelvis ... stomach ... chest ... hands ... wrists ... lower arms ... elbows ... upper arms ... shoulders ... neck ... head. Repeat silently to yourself, 'I am aware I am practising Inner Conscious Relaxation'. For a few moments, watch the incoming and the outgoing breath, breathing naturally.

Now create a resolve, a statement or affirmation (see pages 48–49) that is inspiring and meaningful concerning a change you want to make in your life, one that you know you must fulfil. Use the affirmation suggested on page 71 if you wish. A resolve made in deep relaxation will have a much better chance of manifesting in your life. It is like a seed that you are planting in the garden of your mind. Repeat your resolve three times. At the end of the practice when you read or hear the words 'Peace ... Peace ... Peace', repeat your resolve three more times.

Now systematically rotate your consciousness through your body. As you mentally focus on each part of the body, name it silently and try to visualize that part in your mind. Go slowly.

Right hand thumb ... second finger ... third finger ... fourth finger ... fifth finger ... palm ... wrist ... lower arm ... elbow ... upper arm ... shoulder ... armpit ... waist ... hip ... thigh ... knee ... calf ... ankle ... heel ... sole ... ball of the right foot ... the big toe ... second ... third ... fourth ... fifth toe

toe ... calf ... knee ... thigh ... hip ... waist ... armpit ... shoulder ... upper arm ... elbow ... lower arm ... w

... left hand thumb ... second finger ... third ... fourth ... fifth ... palm ... wrist ... lower arm ... elbow ... upper arm ... shoulder ... armpit ... waist ... hip ... thigh ... knee ... calf ... ankle ... heel ... sole ... ball of the left foot ... the big toe ... second ... third ... fourth ... fifth toe ... right shoulder blade ... left shoulder blade ... spinal cord ... the whole of the back ... left buttock ... right buttock ... genitals ... pelvis ... stomach ... navel ... right chest ... left chest ... centre of the chest ... neck ... chin ... upper lip ... lower lip ... both lips together ... nose ... nose tip ... right cheek ... left cheek ... right temple ... left temple ... right ear ... left ear ... right eye ... left eye ... right eyelid ... left eyelid ... right eyebrow ... left eyebrow ... centre of the eyebrows ... forehead ... top of the head ... back of the head ... whole body ... awareness of the whole body.

Now become aware of any sounds around you, without identifying with any one sound. Simply hear all the sounds simultaneously, from the quietest to the loudest. Stay with this for a few moments. Then bring your awareness directly to your breath. Feel the in and out flow of your breath, the gentle rise and fall of the chest area. Maintain awareness of your breathing for a few moments, without trying to control or change it.

Become aware of your heart and breathe into that area – the heartspace. Visualize a red rose in your heart, a beautiful, many-petalled, half-opened rose. With each breath, let it slowly open more. Feel the soft texture, see the colour, smell the fragrance. Feel that your heart is opening like the petals of the rose.

Peace ... Peace ... Peace. Become aware of the resolve that you made at the beginning of the practice, and repeat it three times to yourself.

Now watch your breathing for a few moments ... move your fingers and toes ... externalize your consciousness. The practice of ICR is over. When you are ready, slowly roll over on to your side, then gently sit up. Have a smile on your face.

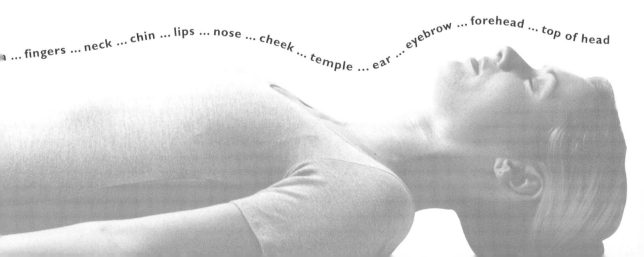

... fingers ... neck ... chin ... lips ... nose ... cheek ... temple ... ear ... eyebrow ... forehead ... top of head

just **breathing** (1 0   m i n u t e s)

Find a comfortable place to sit. Close your eyes and feel your body relaxing. Spend a few moments appreciating your body and the immediate world around you. Now bring your attention to your breath and follow the movement of the breath from the nose, through the chest to the belly, or as deep as you can go. Where do you most feel the breath? Closely observe every detail about the breath from the place where your attention rests, whether at the nose tip, chest or belly. What sensations are you experiencing? Does the breath feel hot or cool? Is it short and quick, or long and slow? Is there a pause after the out breath, or between the inhalation and exhalation? Just watch the breath, observe its natural movement, be aware that you are breathing. Watch one whole breath entering and filling and leaving and emptying ... then watch another ... and then another. When you are ready, gently become aware of your body and of the room around you, and take a deep, full breath.

mantra meditation (2 0   m i n u t e s)

A mantra is a word or sound that we repeat to focus the mind, releasing it from its habitual thinking patterns. Chanting a mantra is remarkably effective at purifying the mind and generating a feeling of peacefulness within. It can be done silently, or out loud if you are alone. It can be practised at any time, anywhere.

Normally, a sacred or religious word or phrase is the most effective mantra. You can use one of the ancient Indian mantras, such as **Om**, which, in Hinduism, represents 'the sound of the universe', **Om Shanthi**, which means 'peace', or a western sacred mantra, such as **Hallelujah**, or **Mother Mary**. A longer mantra is the well-known **Om Mani Padme Hum**, meaning 'the jewel of the awakened mind', or **Om Namah Shivaya**, meaning 'homage to Shiva', the one who transforms negativity of the mind. Or you may prefer to use a sound or short phrase that has meaning for you. Using mantras in Sanskrit or other foreign languages, rather than those in your own, tends to stop the mind from conceptualizing and getting caught up in meaning. It often creates a deeper level of concentration.

the practice Sit in your preferred meditation posture, relax your body and let your breath settle. Then focus on the mantra and begin either to repeat it silently or to intone it out loud. Stay with one mantra for the length of the practice. When using a single-word or two-word mantra, repeat it rhythmically with the in and out breath. Use the mantra to focus the mind so that it can enter into a state of deep absorption. Simply repeat the sound over and over, and let your mind settle into the rhythm.

The mantra acts as an anchor to hold the mind, to bring it to one point. It is a wonderful way of freeing the mind from confusion and doubt, and also of opening your heart. Every time you drift off into thinking or get distracted, just come back to your mantra. All you do is keep repeating that sound over and over, and watch what happens. Observe yourself becoming more and more focused.

In order to deepen concentration in their meditation practice, some people use a mala, a piece of thread strung with either 27 or 108 beads (108 is the number of Hindu names of God, but is also a sacred number that is used in many spiritual traditions). Hold the mala in your right hand and rest the beads on your middle finger. With each recitation of the mantra, use your thumb to move a bead towards you, one at a time. This will help you concentrate on the mantra and the rhythm of the sound. If you time how long it takes you to do one round of the mala, then you will know how many rounds to do for your meditation session and will not need to look at a clock.

lifestyle changes

diet Our normal eating patterns often change when we become stressed. Mealtimes may become irregular; we may eat too little or too much; we may consume nothing but instant food, or lots of carbohydrates in the form of pasties, sandwiches or chips, and eat very little fresh food. This serves only to fuel our stress, as we are not getting the nutrition we need for a balanced physiology. To help you regain a better balance, start to pay greater attention to your food intake, simply noting what you eat, how much and when. For one whole week, write down everything you consume. Notice how you felt before and after you ate. Were you actually hungry, or was it just the 'right' time? Did the food satisfy your needs? Did you notice what you ate? Did you feel hungry again soon afterwards?

This is not the time to judge what you are eating, but simply to develop a greater awareness of your approach to food, and of where your food comes from – how much is fresh and how much is processed. You do not have to change your diet, but as you become more aware of your food intake, you may also notice it changing – awareness itself is transformative.

Also try to become aware of the relationship between your body and the food you eat, and the ways in which your food is yet another vital link between you and the world around you. Your body is dependent on whatever you put inside it, so be aware with each mouthful that you are feeding your muscles, your blood, your brain and your immune system, not just your stomach. Be aware of the person who cooked your food, of the farmer who grew it, of the earth which sustained it, and of the elements which encouraged its growth. Feel how, through your food, you are intimately connected to all life.

attitude Step 1 is about finding that place of safety and belonging within yourself, so take time during this first stage of the programme to feel the ground beneath your feet, to be aware that you walk on the earth, and to appreciate the physical world. In addition, spend time with your family or loved ones and focus on all the good things about them – the places where you relate, the fun you have together and the love that you share. Make a point of doing something to help a family member or close friend.

mirroring self

To develop a greater acceptance of yourself, try this powerful exercise. It is not easy, at least not to begin with, but the more you do it the more effective it is. You do not have to attempt it all at once – go slowly and be gentle and loving with yourself.

Take about 10–15 minutes every day to stand naked in front of a mirror (making sure that you will not be disturbed!). Very slowly go over each part of your body, one bit at a time. Avoid making a judgement about the overall image. Instead, just look at one knee or one thigh or one lock of hair at a time, slowly covering your whole body. Try to see it just as it is, without the judgemental, critical mind taking over. There is an inherent beauty, a natural loveliness that is in all life if we look with an open heart.

Quietly say, 'I love you', to each part of your body. This may feel strange at first, and you may not even feel very loving, but continue anyway and watch what happens. As you do this exercise each day, you will develop an attitude to your body that will make you feel much more at peace with yourself.

2

relating to
relationship

How we treat others and the world around us directly reflects how we feel about ourselves. When we feel inwardly secure and at home with ourselves, we will naturally have more respect and care for others and for our world; whereas if we are uneasy or insecure within ourselves, then either we will be more easily influenced and subject to others' opinions, or we will be dismissive and uncaring to anyone or anything that gets in our way. In Step 2 we develop awareness of our relationships – and in the process learn more about ourselves – by observing how we relate to others. This is the area of the second chakra.

Begin by examining how you behave with others. Are you the dominant or the passive partner? Do you express yourself honestly or do you hide your feelings behind pleasantries? Do you give less or more than you get? Do you listen to the other person, and do you feel heard? Are you maintaining relationships that do not feel nourishing or caring? And if so, can you see why?

Relationship…is the mirror in which you discover yourself. Without relationship you are not; to be is to be related; to be related is existence. You exist only in relationship; otherwise you do not exist; existence has no meaning.

KRISHNAMURTI

In particular, begin to recognize how your desires influence the ways in which you communicate and interact with others. Without this self-knowledge, we will continue simply to react to people and events, and our responses will invariably be filled with hidden agendas, such as unfulfilled needs, expectations and presumptions. Desires occupy our minds with a constant craving for more, whether it is for more acknowledgement, love or compatibility, or for greater power, prestige or recognition. With a better awareness of our deep-seated motivations, we can learn to respond rather than react; and when we can communicate without our own needs overpowering us, our relationships will be more open and honest.

Watch your reactions to others, especially when difficulties arise, or when you feel let down, hurt, unloved, put upon, doubted or confronted. As you come away from such an

Love in the past is only a memory. Love in the future is a fantasy. Only here and now can we truly love. THE BUDDHA

encounter, notice what is happening inside you. Did you anticipate that you would get more than you received? Did you feel that you were not being recognized or appreciated? Did the other person not live up to your standards or expectations? Did you try to control or dominate the conversation? Did you feel used or dismissed as unimportant? Did you feel your needs were not being met?

I am received with understanding and love by all beings, and I receive all beings with wisdom and compassion.

When you have identified your unspoken desires, replay the entire incident in your mind without those expectations and see how different it looks. From this more objective stance, can you see how your subjective needs can cause conflict and misunderstanding? It is only with this understanding that you can begin to value the importance of staying centred no matter what is going on.

There is nothing either good nor bad, but thinking makes it so. WILLIAM SHAKESPEARE

Our relationships are not just with people, they are also with the world around us. When we are stressed we forget the beauty of simple things; we become distanced, uncaring or even hostile. We take less care of our possessions, throwing things away when they no longer serve us, rather than taking time to repair or recycle them. Then we begin to desire more things, in the belief that they will serve us better. See where you can be more aware of your environment and your relationships and where you can bring more concern and responsibility towards other people.

stretching (15–20 minutes)

Take a moment to stretch up and open your body, then repeat Standing Pose in Step 1 (see page 72).

The following exercises will loosen your whole body, releasing tension and stiffness.

heavenly stretch

❶ Stay in the standing position with your feet a few inches apart and, keeping your head facing forwards, stretch and point your hands up to the sky. Have your eyes focused on a static point in front of you.

❷ Gently come up on your toes, feeling the stretch from your toes to your finger-tips, all the way up your body. Stay like this for as long as you feel comfortable, then gently open your arms out to the sides and come back down. Repeat twice more.

arm swing

❶ Have your feet facing forwards the same distance apart as your shoulders. Keeping your back and head straight, bend your knees to a position that you can hold comfortably. Breathe in and out from your belly.

❷ Keeping your knees bent and your arms relaxed, swing your arms around your body from side to side, rotating your head and torso with each swing. Turn only from the waist up and keep your hips and knees facing forwards. Feel the spine opening and loosening with each turn. Keep breathing while you move. Let your hands slap your body as you turn, the motion getting bigger or faster as feels comfortable. Continue for as long as you want, aiming for at least 30 turns. Then gently slow your arms down and just stand still for a moment, breathing.

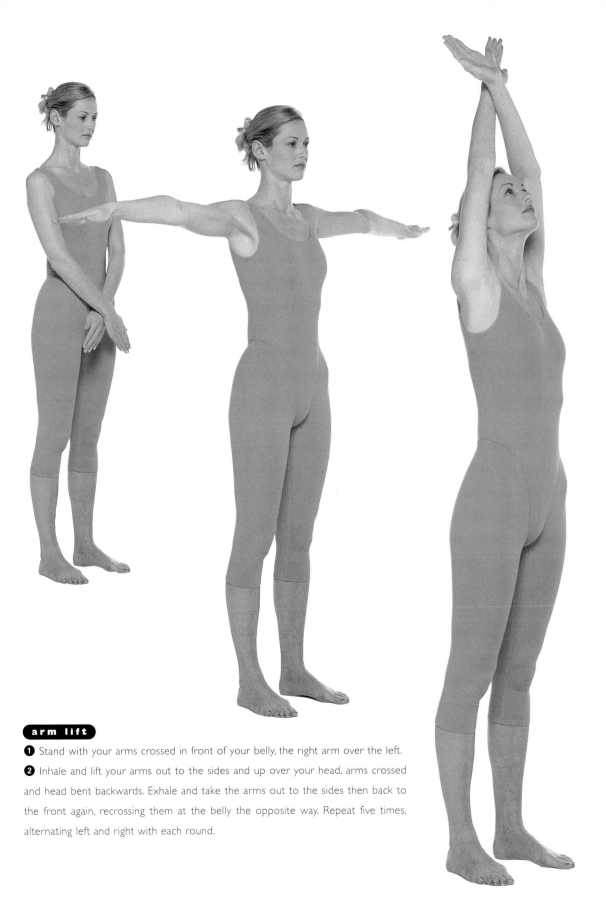

arm lift

❶ Stand with your arms crossed in front of your belly, the right arm over the left.

❷ Inhale and lift your arms out to the sides and up over your head, arms crossed and head bent backwards. Exhale and take the arms out to the sides then back to the front again, recrossing them at the belly the opposite way. Repeat five times, alternating left and right with each round.

2

side stretch

❶ Now take your feet about two to three feet apart. Stretch your arms out to the sides.

❷ Gently bend to the right side, letting the right arm rest on your leg while the left arm is stretched straight up above the head, palm facing to the right. Turn your head as far as you can to look up at the palm.

❸ Now look down at the right hand as you lift it up and over to the left side. The left hand rests on the left leg while the right arm is raised upwards, palm facing to the left, head looking up at the palm. Repeat five times on each side, breathing with the movement.

forwards bend

❶ With your feet just a few inches apart, inhale and stretch your arms all the way up to the ceiling.

❷ Bend forwards as you exhale, moving from the waist, with your head coming last. Place your hands on the floor beside your feet or hold your legs where you can reach comfortably. Let your torso relax forward, relax your neck and head, keep your knees soft – they can even bend a little if you like. The object here is to relax and open the spine, not to hurt your legs. Take a few breaths in this downward position, and with each breath feel your spine opening more.

❸ When you are ready, breathe in and *slowly* lift up from the waist. Take your arms up and over your head and let your head fall backwards and your spine arch gently in a reverse pose. Then come back to a standing position, arms at your sides, and be still for a few moments.

running Finally, to loosen your whole body, gently start to run on the spot. Keep breathing and moving. Feel your whole body begin to relax and soften. Keep running in one place for as long as it feels comfortable. Then stop, take a deep breath and stand still for a few moments, allowing your breath to settle.

Now prepare yourself for Inner Conscious Relaxation.

inner **conscious relaxation** (15–20 minutes)

Find a comfortable position lying down. Take a deep breath and blow it out. Relax your body by bringing awareness to your toes and working your way up, releasing tension in the feet ... legs ... back of the body ... chest ... hands ... arms ... shoulders ... neck ... head. Repeat silently to yourself, 'I am aware I am practising Inner Conscious Relaxation'. Watch incoming and outgoing breath, breathing naturally, for a few moments. Now create your resolve, the statement or affirmation concerning your life that is inspiring or meaningful to you. Use the affirmation suggested on page 83 if you wish. Repeat this three times. At the end of the practice when you read or hear the words 'Peace ... Peace ... Peace', repeat your resolve three more times.

Now systematically rotate your consciousness through your body. As you mentally focus on each part of the body, name it silently and also try to visualize that part in your mind. Go slowly.

Right hand thumb ... second finger ... third finger ... fourth finger ... fifth finger ... palm ... wrist ... lower arm ... elbow ... upper arm ... shoulder ... armpit ... waist ... hip ... thigh ... knee ... calf ... ankle ... heel ... sole ... ball of the right foot ... the big toe ... second ... third ... fourth ... fifth toe ... left hand thumb ... second finger ... third ... fourth ... fifth ... palm ... wrist ... lower arm ... elbow ... upper arm ... shoulder ... armpit ... waist ... hip ... thigh ... knee ... calf ... ankle ... heel ... sole ... ball of the left foot ... the big toe ... second ... third ... fourth ... fifth toe ... right shoulder blade ... left shoulder blade ... spinal cord ... the whole of the back ... left buttock ... right buttock ... genitals ... pelvis ... stomach ... navel ... right chest ... left chest ... centre of the chest ... neck ... chin ... upper lip ... lower lip ... both lips together ... nose ... nose tip ... right cheek ... left cheek ... right temple ... left temple ... right ear ... left ear ... right eye ... left eye ... right eyelid ... left eyelid ... right eyebrow ... left eyebrow ... centre of the eyebrows ... forehead ... top of the head ... back of the head ... whole body ... awareness of the whole body.

toe ... calf ... knee ... thigh ... hip ... waist ... armpit ... shoulder ... upper arm ... elbow ... lower arm ... w

Maintain awareness of your breathing for a few moments. Now become aware of the contact between your body and the ground beneath you. Bring your attention to whatever part of your body comes into contact with the floor, beginning with your right leg and the ground. Become aware of the point of contact and focus your attention on that space.

Now be aware of the point of contact of your left leg and the ground ... stay with your awareness there for a few moments ... then of your right arm and the ground ... maintain awareness of that space ... of your left arm and the ground ... bring your attention to that space.

Now focus on the point of contact of your buttocks and the ground ... have awareness of the meeting point and the space. ... your back and the ground ... stay with this for a few moments. Now bring your attention to the meeting point between your head and the ground ... of the whole of your physical body and the ground ... get closer to the awareness of this space.

Now visualize your body as a temple. You are in this temple for the whole of your life. Know that it is a blessing, a gift that you have received. It is in this form, within this temple, that you find your essence, your peace, freedom. Honour your body as a precious place. Then bring your awareness to your breath, that which gives life to this temple. Stay with your breath for a few moments.

Peace ... Peace ... Peace. Become aware of the resolve that you made at the beginning of the practice, and repeat it three times to yourself.

Become aware of your breathing ... of the room you are in ... move your fingers and toes ... externalize your consciousness. The practice of ICR is over. When you are ready, slowly roll over onto your side, then gently sit up. Have a smile on your face.

... fingers ... neck ... chin ... lips ... nose ... cheek ... temple ... ear ... eyebrow ... forehead ... top of head

nature walk (10 minutes)

If possible, start your evening programme with a walk out in the open – whether it is in a town park, through a wood or by a canal. (Choose somewhere you will feel comfortable and safe walking alone.) Make this time an opportunity simply to look and appreciate what you see. Enjoy the colours and the shapes, the smells and the sounds that are all around you. Watch the birds or the animals, the trees or the water. Open yourself to the beauty of the natural world. If it is raining, enjoy the feeling of rain drops falling on your face, appreciate how the water is nourishing the earth and the plants; if it is windy, marvel at the power of nature, of a force that is beyond our control; if it is cloudy, observe the subtle colours of the clouds and the softness of the air. Recognize that we need the nourishment of the earth, the plants, the sun, the wind and the rain.

appreciation
meditation (20 minutes)

Normally we take so much for granted and spend very little time in simple appreciation. We may love flowers and beautiful objects, but it is unusual to extend our gratitude to the chair we are sitting on, to the people who made it, or to the food we eat or the farmers who grew and harvested it. Yet when we do it extends and opens us beyond ourselves, we feel humbled, grateful and enriched, and we are reminded yet again of how interconnected we all are. In the meditation you slowly expand your awareness from yourself to your seat, to the room and then outwards to the world around you, linking with everything that is sustaining and supporting you. Soon you realize that there is nothing that does not contribute to your life.

the practice Find a comfortable meditation posture. Take a deep breath as you settle your body. Begin by developing a deep appreciation and gratitude for the cushion or chair that you are sitting on. Thank it for supporting you in your practice. Honour the people who made your seat, and thank all the elements that were involved in the making of the wood, upholstery and so on.

Now extend your appreciation to the building around you. Feel gratitude for its protection and safety, and for the space it provides in which you can meditate.

Silently thank those who designed the building, the materials used in its construction, and the team of people who built it. Now extend your appreciation to the ground beneath you, which is always there, supporting and sustaining you throughout your life. Feel a deep gratitude for the earth, home to everyone and everything. Be thankful for the trees and the plants, the animals and the birds, the oceans and the fish. Offer your gratitude to the sky above, to the sun that brings warmth, to the moon and stars that lighten the darkness, and the clouds that bring sweet rain.

Now extend your gratitude to your body, appreciating how it serves you, and how it is a vessel through which you experience love, joy and unconditional happiness. Honour the fact that your body is dependent on the food that you eat, the water that you drink and the air that you breathe. Respect that it needs to be clothed, and how the fabrics that make up your garments started life as either a plant or an animal. Acknowledge how your physical body is connected to all the elements.

Now extend your appreciation to your parents, for without them you would not be here, would not have this body, and would not be sitting in meditation, opening your heart in appreciation. Honour what they gave you, however little, as being the most of which they were capable. Then extend that gratitude further back, to your grandparents and distant ancestors. Between them all they gave you the colour of your hair, the shape of your eyes, the laughter in your voice. They passed on to you their experience and insights, that you may grow greater than them. Acknowledge that their bodies have now returned to the earth, completing cycles of interdependency, each feeding and nourishing the other.

From your ancestors slowly expand outwards, feeling your connection with all beings. See how we all walk this earth together, breathing the same air. See each one as a spark of light, sometimes ablaze, sometimes dim, each light reflecting all the other lights.

Now bring your appreciation and gratitude back to yourself and your breath. Become aware of the flow of your breath entering and leaving your body. We cannot own this breath – it is ours not to keep but to share. Spend a few moments appreciating your breath and the life it brings to you. Take that appreciation with you into your daily life.

lifestyle changes

diet Throughout Step 2, make fruit and fruit juices an important part of your daily diet. Try having a large mixed fruit salad and a glass of fresh juice for breakfast, and fruit as a snack throughout the day, or as a starter before your main meal in the evening. For just one day a week, try eating nothing but fruit for the whole day – as much as you like of whatever fruit you prefer, with a minimum of one banana a day, – and drink lots of fresh juice. You can also drink herb teas on this day, but no caffeine or alcohol. This has a wonderful cleansing effect and will help flush out toxins that have built up in your system. To prepare your system for a fruit-only day, have a light meal the evening before – perhaps a clear vegetable soup and a baked potato. A post fruit-fast menu could be fruit for breakfast, soup or salad for lunch, and an evening meal of grilled fish or tofu and vegetables, with brown rice or a baked potato.

WARNING: A few people may experience some side-effects from detoxification on a fruit-only day. (If you are a heavy coffee or tea drinker, it is probably best not to do this until you have reduced your intake to two cups a day or less.) The symptoms of detoxification can be an upset stomach or a headache. Although these can be uncomfortable, they are a good sign: they mean your body is cleansing itself. Your body is also telling you that your current diet probably contains too many processed and/or sugary foods. Simply drink plenty of water and lie down for a while, and the symptoms will pass. If you are in any doubt as to whether you should follow a day's fruit fast, consult your doctor first.

attitude Each day, spend just a few minutes focusing on what is really important in your life. See if you can make a list of your priorities. Are they material success? Prestige or control at work? Well-behaved children? Or are they to go hiking in the hills? To play and share time with your loved ones? To express your creativity or feelings? To be at peace with yourself? Discover what is most important to you, what is really meaningful and enriching, and then learn to let go of what you don't need.

insight on relationships

This exercise will help you to have a better understanding of a close relationship, and particularly where it goes wrong and why. When you do this, fill in the blanks with the person's name. This is a chance to observe the relationship objectively and see whether the difficulties lie with you or with them, and what improvements need to be made.

Find a quiet place to be alone. Have paper and a pen with you. Start by breathing deeply and relaxing your whole body. Then slowly let the other person come into your mind. Let them be there and become aware of any feelings that arise, whether those feelings are loving or not. Do not judge. Spend a few minutes looking back over your shared history. Remember the good times and the not so good. See if there is a pattern to the development of this relationship. Stay with your feelings as you explore all aspects of it. When you are ready, ask yourself these questions:

★ Do I feel supported and nourished by ....?

★ Am I being supportive and nourishing of ....?

★ Do I feel listened to or heard by ....?

★ Am I honest when I express my feelings?

★ Do I listen and really hear ....?

★ Do we trust each other?

★ What would I most like to change in the relationship?

★ What is needed for this change to happen?

★ How am I contributing to maintaining this relationship?

★ In what ways can I take more responsibility for my contribution?

★ How is my behaviour affecting ....?

★ Beneath any difficulties, what do I really feel about ....?

★ Have I shared these feelings?

★ Have I said 'I love you' today?

Take your time to answer these questions, and ask yourself any others to which you feel you need answers. When you have finished, sit quietly for a few minutes and let your answers speak to you.

discovering
personal power

In Step 3 we begin to develop a deeper feeling of our self-worth and self-esteem. We discover our personal power and potency. However, it is important to make a distinction here. Personal power is not having power over someone or something else – it does not involve manipulation or control, competition or conquest. It is not a self-centred or egotistical state, where we are only concerned with ourselves, our needs, or our influence over others. Nor does it involve proving our worth through the accumulation of wealth and material possessions, political authority or business acumen.

Personal power arises from self-knowledge, from a bond of friendship with and love of ourselves. Beyond that it moves to an awareness of our fundamental kinship with all beings. We are able to claim our own feelings and thoughts, without excluding the validity of someone else's beliefs; we know our weaknesses, while honouring

He who knows much about others may be learned, but he who understands himself is more intelligent. He who controls others may be powerful, but he who has mastered himself is mightier still. LAO TZU

our strengths. This is the measure of a positive ego, where self-confidence and a healthy sense of self sustain us no matter what happens in our lives. Personal power emerges from that place where self-worth, interconnectedness, inner strength and a sense of belonging all meet. This is the area of the third chakra, that of a growing inner authority.

However, in order for our inner potency to develop we may first have to confront and overcome our fears and limitations, and to embrace those parts of ourselves that pull back or cower, that are timid, nervous or apprehensive. We may also need to overcome a fear of being seen or

Do your duty always, but without attachment. That is how a man reaches the ultimate Truth; by working without anxiety about results. BHAGAVAD GITA

intimately known by others, or feelings of worthlessness or inadequacy. For in these ways we give our power away. We let others lead us or determine how we should think and feel, becoming dependent on them for our well-being; or we blame ourselves when anything goes wrong, quick to believe we must be the one at fault, rather than seeing we are only a part of the picture. Step 3 is about recognizing these tendencies and having greater compassion for our humanity, seeing that there is no need to hold on to self-blame, shame and guilt. Our worthiness is not dependent on what we do, but rather on our innate beauty.

I know myself to be a worthy and beautiful being, and I have the resources and inner strength to do or be anything I choose.

In this way we move from being a victim to being a victor, not over anyone else, but in our own minds, in the way that we think about ourselves. The victim mind-set has no personal power, no self-esteem or inner certitude; rather, it sees others as the enemy and the self as the loser. The victor mentality recognizes the fundamental equality between all beings, and truly embraces the notion that no-one is higher or more powerful than another, that we are all here together to support and love one another. With this insight we can maintain our integrity and emotional stability, while participating fully in life. To be a victor we do not need power or control over others – it is enough to know ourselves.

> **Stay centred, do not overstretch. Extend from your centre, return to your centre.** MASTER MIAN

Developing personal power increases our sensitivity and awareness, not only to ourselves, but also to others. Our intuition tells us what others are feeling, even if those feelings are unexpressed. We become more finely attuned to the unspoken and the unacknowledged, thus gaining greater insight into the nature of what it is to be fully human. In turn, this generates greater compassion for all beings.

> **Not once in a thousand times is it possible to achieve anything worth achieving except by labour, by effort, by serious purpose and by willingness to take risks.** THEODORE ROOSEVELT

discovering personal power

95

stretching and breathing

(15–20 minutes)

Start by running on the spot and loosening your whole body. Feel any tightness from the night beginning to release and relax. Take a deep breath and blow it out.

upper body stretch

❶ With your feet a few inches apart, stretch both arms up towards the ceiling and join hands, palms facing upwards. On an out breath, bend to the right; breathe in as you return to an upright position, and breathe out as you bend to the left. Repeat three times on each side. Then relax with your arms by your sides.

❷ Stretch both arms up again and, on an out breath, bend forwards from the waist, letting your whole spine gently uncurl and open. Let yourself hang for a moment, then take a deep breath and unfold upwards.

swinging pose

This posture not only releases the spine, but also all the stale air from your lungs. WARNING: Do not practise this if you have high blood pressure. Instead, stand and breathe deeply for a few minutes, with your chest open and your arms stretched back.

❶ Stand with your feet a few feet apart – the wider your feet the easier this exercise is. Breathe in and stretch your arms up above your head.

❷ Blow the breath out as you swing down from the waist, your arms going between your legs.

❸ Without coming all the way up to an upright position, lift and swing your arms between your legs four more times while breathing in deeply as you come up and out as you come down.

❹ Return to the upright position, arms above your head. Take a breath. Then repeat the whole movement twice more. Then stand and relax for a few moments.

leg warmers

1 Lie down on your back with your arms by your sides and take a moment to relax. Keeping the left leg straight, on an in breath raise the right leg straight up in the air, supporting it with hands clasped behind the thigh if you need to. (If you have a bad back, bend your left leg and keep your left foot flat on the floor.)

2 Point your right foot, feeling the leg muscles stretching, then circle the right leg clockwise ten times. Slowly bring the right leg back to the floor.

3 Repeat with the left leg.

4 Now lift both legs up, using your hands to support your buttocks if necessary. Then open them to the sides as far as you can go, supporting your thighs with your hands. Breathe in this pose for a moment, feeling the stretch on the inner thighs.

5 Gently come back to the centre and bring your legs back to the ground. Take a deep breath and relax for a moment.

pranayama alternate breathing *There are many different ways we can use the breath to balance the nerves and calm our whole being. This is a traditional yoga breathing exercise that has been used for hundreds of years. Prana is the vital force, the essence of life, that is in all things; yama is to control or direct, indicating that we can control or increase the prana to stimulate the energy within us and bring greater well-being.*

❶ Sit cross-legged on the floor, or sit on a chair with a straight back. Take a few deep breaths as you settle. Then, using either your right or left hand, rest your thumb beside one nostril, your index and middle fingers in the space between your eyebrows (where they stay throughout the practice), and the last two fingers beside the other nostril. Close your eyes.

❷ If using your right hand, close your right nostril with your thumb, inhale through the left nostril, then close the left nostril with your two last fingers, open the right nostril and breathe out through it. Then breathe in through the right, close the right and open the left nostril and breathe out through the left. Then open both nostrils and breathe in and out. This is one round.

❸ Continue doing this, with your eyes closed, for five rounds. When you have finished, put your hand down, take a deep breath, and sit quietly for a few moments before beginning your meditation.

As you feel more comfortable with this exercise, begin to equalize the length of each inhalation and exhalation by counting the length. Aim for five counts each. Or you can silently repeat Om with each in and out breath.

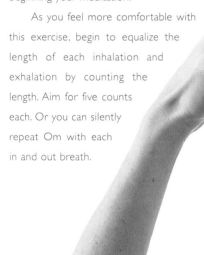

inner conscious relaxation (15–20 minutes)

Find a comfortable position lying down. Take a deep breath and blow it out. Relax your body by bringing awareness to your toes and working your way up, releasing tension in the feet ... legs ... back of the body ... chest ... hands ... arms ... shoulders ... neck ... head. Repeat silently to yourself, 'I am aware I am practising Inner Conscious Relaxation'. Watch incoming and outgoing breath, breathing naturally, for a few moments. Now create your resolve, the statement or affirmation concerning your life that is inspiring or meaningful to you. Use the affirmation suggested on page 95 if you wish. Repeat this three times. At the end of the practice when you read or hear the words 'Peace ... Peace ... Peace', repeat your resolve three more times.

Now systematically rotate your consciousness through your body. As you mentally focus on each part of the body, name it silently and also try to visualize that part in your mind. Go slowly.

Right hand thumb ... second finger ... third finger ... fourth finger ... fifth finger ... palm ... wrist ... lower arm ... elbow ... upper arm ... shoulder ... armpit ... waist ... hip ... thigh ... knee ... calf ... ankle ... heel ... sole ... ball of the right foot ... the big toe ... second ... third ... fourth ... fifth toe ... left hand thumb ... second finger ... third ... fourth ... fifth ... palm ... wrist ... lower arm ... elbow ... upper arm ... shoulder ... armpit ... waist ... hip ... thigh ... knee ... calf ... ankle ... heel ... sole ... ball of the left foot ... the big toe ... second ... third ... fourth ... fifth toe ... right shoulder blade ... left shoulder blade ... spinal cord ... the whole of the back ... left buttock ... right buttock ... genitals ... pelvis ... stomach ... navel ... right chest ... left chest ... centre of the chest ... neck ... chin ... upper lip ... lower lip ... both lips together ... nose ... nose tip ... right cheek ... left cheek ... right temple ... left temple ... right ear ... left ear ... right eye ... left eye ... right eyelid ... left eyelid ... right eyebrow ... left eyebrow ... centre of the eyebrows ... forehead ... top of the head ... back of the head ... whole body ... awareness of the whole body.

toe ... calf ... knee ... thigh ... hip ... waist ... armpit ... shoulder ... upper arm ... elbow ... lower arm ...

Maintain awareness of your breathing for a few moments. Now begin to focus on opposite sensations, heaviness, lightness, coldness and heat. First, create a feeling of heaviness in your body ... feel that your legs are getting heavier ... your buttocks ... back ... arms ... chest ... head ... your whole body is feeling heavy, as if it is sinking down into the ground. Stay with this for a few moments. Now create a feeling of lightness ... bring lightness to your body ... to your fingers ... arms ... stomach ... chest ... back ... legs ... shoulders ... neck ... your whole body is light, as if you are floating off the ground. Stay with this for a few moments.

Now create a feeling of coldness in your body ... in your hands ... feet ... buttocks ... feel a chill up your spine ... your whole body is getting colder. You are walking in the snow. Stay with this for a few moments. Now create the feeling of heat ... in your hands ... in your right foot ... left foot ... in your stomach ... chest ... lips ... in your whole body. You are in the desert ... the midday sun is beating down above ... feel the heat. Stay with this for a few moments.

Now we move to the next phase of the practice, visualization. Imagine you are lying on a beach, the sun warming your body, the waves gently lapping at your feet. Breathe in the salty smell of the water, hear the waves breaking, feel the hot sand beneath your body, hear the birds calling. Feel any tension or concerns ebbing away with each wave, until you have completely surrendered to the moment.

Peace ... Peace ... Peace. Become aware of the resolve that you made at the beginning of the practice, and repeat it three times to yourself.

Now watch your breathing for a few moments ... move your fingers and toes ... externalize your consciousness. The practice of ICR is over. When you are ready, slowly roll over on to your side, then gently sit up. Have a smile on your face.

... fingers ... neck ... chin ... lips ... nose ... cheek ... temple ... ear ... eyebrow ... forehead ... top of head

fast **walking** (10 minutes)

Fast walking loosens every part of your body, releases old, stale air from the lungs, and invigorates your circulation and nervous system – an excellent activity after a day at work. It can be done anywhere, at any time, in any weather. Do it around your house or outside, in bare feet or in shoes, whichever you prefer. Wear loose, comfortable clothing and walk fast, but with awareness. Have your hands by your sides, or bend your arms at your elbows and move them with your stride. You may even swing your arms up and down with each stride. Breathe as you walk. Feel your whole body loosening and releasing. Let this be an energizing and uplifting exercise. Sing as you walk! Chant Om as you walk! Walk fast but rhythmically and enjoy your body moving.

When you have finished, stand absolutely still for a moment and close your eyes. Simply breathe and feel the energy moving in your body. See how different you feel from when you started.

breath awareness
meditation~1 (30 minutes)

This meditation is one of the oldest, most well-used and deeply effective meditations used throughout all spiritual traditions; it is also very simple and easy to practise. Its very simplicity is why it is so effective. If 30 minutes is too much for you to do at once, start with 15 minutes and gradually increase the amount of time as you feel more familiar and at ease with the practice. You are not going to achieve anything by sitting there for the full 30 minutes if you feel uncomfortable.

Choose your preferred seated meditation position and sit with your back straight. Take a deep breath and let it out through your mouth as you settle your body. Spend a few moments appreciating your seat, the ground beneath you, your body, and your breath.

With this exercise your breath is completely natural: it is neither short nor long, slow nor fast. Awareness is on the flow of the breath as it comes into the body and leaves again. Rest your attention either in the belly, approximately two inches below the navel, or in the centre of your chest at the heartspace, or where the breath enters at the nose tip, whichever place feels most comfortable and natural to you.

the practice Start by silently counting your breaths at the end of each out breath: breathe in, breathe out, count one; breathe in, breathe out, two; breathe in, breathe out, three. Continue counting in this way until you get to ten, then start at one again.

At any time, if you lose count, or you find you are counting beyond ten, bring your attention back and start at one again. The counting acts as an anchor so that your mind stays focused on the breath. Stay in the present by breathing just one breath fully ... then another ... then another.

The mind is easily distracted and disturbed, and will want to go off in all different directions. As it arises, label each thought 'thinking' and then let it go, like a bird flying away in the sky. Always return to the counting. Thoughts are bound to come, but if you do not attach yourself to them, they will soon settle. Your mind will become quieter as you focus more deeply on your breath and internalize your attention. Simply watch the natural flow of the breath and the movement of your body without making any conscious changes. Each time your mind drifts bring it back. Let yourself sink ever deeper into the breath.

After about ten minutes, change to counting at the beginning of each in breath: count one, breathe in, breathe out; two, breathe in, breathe out; three, breathe in, breathe out, and so on, up to ten, and then start at one again. This shifts the focus of your concentration from awareness of the breath after you have breathed, to becoming aware of the breath before it enters the body. This deepens your concentration and enables you to enter the quiet mind even further.

After another ten minutes you can stop counting the breath and simply watch the movement of your body and the breath as you inhale and exhale. Stay with each breath, experiencing it fully, and then breathing the next one. If you find it difficult to focus like this, continue with the counting.

After a further ten minutes, take a deep breath, become aware of the seat beneath you, the room you are in and the world around you. Gently open your eyes and have a good stretch.

lifestyle changes

diet Step 3 is about developing personal power, and we can also extend this to what we buy and eat. Everything we consume has an effect on our health and well-being, and it is up to us to educate ourselves as to what is good for us and what may harm us. We are not victims of the food industry – we do not have to buy something just because it is on the shelf. We can make healthy and informed choices and these will influence the market as a whole. For instance, buy local food wherever possible to support local business; buy organic produce to reduce chemical intake and to support small farmers; cut down on fats and fast foods wherever possible; buy whole grains and wholewheat bread rather than white rice, flour or bread; reduce red meat consumption and increase the amount of vegetables, tofu, nuts and seeds you eat; buy from countries practising fair trading and avoid those that exploit their workers; read the list of ingredients on the labels and try to avoid preservatives, colourings, sugar or artificial sweeteners; take your own bags when you go shopping rather than getting new carriers, and support small local shops rather than large supermarkets. In this way we can assert ourselves as consumers while generating greater awareness of the importance of what we eat and our relationship to food.

attitude Throughout Step 3 develop an attitude of openness, of possibility. Notice each time you hear yourself saying, 'I must...', 'I ought to...', or 'I should...'. Rather than behaving how you think you ought to behave, look inside yourself and see what you are really feeling, what your own beliefs and attitudes are, and how you can most creatively express yourself. Discover spontaneity and freedom of choice. This means learning to dance to the beat of your own drum, to find your own way of doing things.

tuning in

This exercise is deceptively simple to practise – all you have to do is not turn on the television! This may not be easy – old habits die hard – so start with one day at a time and see what happens. Your objective is to develop greater personal resources, which is very difficult if your free time is spent sitting in front of a black box with flashing lights, watching pictures move before your eyes.

To gain personal power requires us to develop a sense of our own creativity and capabilities. Do you remember all the things you loved to do as a child, or the dreams you had of what you would do when you grew up? Now is your chance to do all those things. Try spending each day or evening when you would be watching television or reading the paper doing something you wouldn't normally attempt: take a class in painting, dancing or singing, go for a long walk or a swim, listen to music, read an inspiring book, learn a musical instrument, write your biography. Or simply spend time being quiet within yourself, appreciating the beauty of your own being.

4
opening
the heart

Self-worth, relationships and personal power are amongst life's most precious jewels, but they are only made meaningful in the presence of love, for it is love that overcomes all difficulties, releases all pain and transports us beyond our limitations. Step 4 is about opening the heart – the centre of love – so that we can discover the depth, power and magnitude of the love that is always within us and bring it alive in our lives. For love is not something that can be found outside us, it comes from within, from the very core or essence of our being. This is the realm of the heart chakra.

Yet despite its transformative power, many of us are frightened of love, or are reticent about showing our loving feelings for fear of appearing foolish. Our culture is so dominated by the mind that matters of the heart are rarely discussed or shared, and we are not taught to honour or respect the heart's longing to express love. Rather, we

Ultimately your greatest teacher is to live with an open heart. EMMANUEL

believe that love is something we get from others, or that must be earned and of which we must be worthy. We believe that if we are not loved it is because there is something wrong with us, that in some way we are not lovable. We do not realize that the love we receive from others is far less than the love already there inside each of us, that we each have a heart filled with love.

The love we seek to awaken, or rediscover, is the love that is unconditional, that cannot be turned on and off or directed only to a few. Opening the heart is about accessing the love that goes beyond the ego, beyond our own needs and personal preferences. It is the love that fully acknowledges that there is pain and accepts the reality of suffering, but does not let that diminish our capacity for loving. With love, we can move away from selfishness and self-centredness and open ourselves to selflessness, generosity and compassion.

Just for a moment, right now, stop reading and breathe into your heart by focusing your attention and awareness in the centre of your chest – the area we call the heartspace. Watch the breath from that place, and try to feel as if you are breathing in and out of your

It's about walking through the world of fear so that you can live in a world of love. BRUCE SPRINGSTEEN

heart. Do this for a few minutes. At first you may find you experience a tightness there, a bit like an ache, or even a feeling of sadness, but as you continue with your breathing it will soften and release any pain that is held there to reveal the love that is its true expression.

I open my heart to the love, forgiveness, mercy and compassion that form its true nature, and I share that love with all beings equally.

Throughout Step 4 your focus is on extending love both to yourself and to all others. To live with an open heart is to accept our humanity and vulnerability. When we live with love as our guide, we can see beyond our differences and difficulties to the place where we all meet. Opening the heart heals the pain of separation, and the love that emerges is like the sun that shines equally on all.

Awakening the heart brings forth our compassion and mercy, a loving kindness that does not judge or reject. This does not mean that we should become like door-mats, so nice and easy-going that we let everyone walk all over us! An open heart is one that gives and loves with awareness; it sees clearly and acts in a way that is most appropriate to each situation. It goes beyond the content to recognizing the essence.

The heart is like a garden. It can grow compassion or fear, resentment or love. What seeds will you plant there?

THE BUDDHA

With love we find our peace. It is the missing piece of the jigsaw puzzle, the one quality that balances all others. With it comes a deep inner joy, equanimity, gentleness and grace. Let these qualities begin to fill your being.

stretching (15 minutes)

Start by spending a few minutes running on the spot, loosening your whole body, and easing out any tensions and tightness. Stretch your arms up and down and then out to the sides, swing one leg at a time back and forth and round in circles. When you feel really loose, lie down on the floor, flat on your back, preferably on a mat or folded blanket.

knees to chest *This exercise helps to relax the pelvis and releases any tension in the abdominal area.*

❶ Bring your knees to your chest and put one hand on each knee. Take each knee out to the side (let your feet fall naturally together in the middle) and slowly rotate them three times clockwise, and then three times anticlockwise.

❷ Bring your knees back to the centre of your chest and clasp your hands around them. Breathe in, and on an out breath lift your head to your knees, hold it there for a moment, then breathe in as you lower your head back to the floor. Repeat this five times.

spinal twist

This exercise gives the spine a good stretch, relaxing the central nervous system.

❶ Bend your knees, keeping your feet flat on the ground behind your buttocks. Stretch your arms out to the sides, at the same level as your shoulders, with the palms facing down.

❷ On an out breath, gently lower your knees to the floor on your left while your head turns to face your right hand, creating a spinal twist. Only take your knees as far left as feels comfortable, but try to keep both shoulder blades in contact with the floor.

❸ On an in breath, bring your knees back to the centre and, on the next out breath, let the knees go to the floor on your right as your head turns to face your left hand. This is one round.

❹ Continue for a further five rounds. You can move with each breath or, if you feel comfortable, stay in each position for a few breaths. Feel the stretch in your spine and hips. If you wish to stretch further, straighten your legs and stretch your feet out to meet your hand on each side.

opening the heart

4

The next two exercises are excellent for strengthening the spine and releasing the abdominal muscles.

rowing a boat

❶ Stretch out on the ground and relax for a moment. When you are ready, sit up with your legs straight in front of you with your feet together.

❷ With your arms moving as if rowing a boat, bend the body forwards as far as possible, then backwards as far as you can comfortably without your back touching the ground, then forwards again over your legs (see below).

❸ Continue moving backwards and forwards for five strokes.

❹ Then reverse the movement, as if rowing backwards, and repeat five times.

grinding flour

❶ Stay in the same position as for Rowing a Boat above, but this time with your legs two feet apart and your arms stretched in front of you, fingers interlocked with knuckles facing outwards.

❷ Make a horizontal circular movement from the waist, as if grinding flour. Move in a large circle, reaching as far forwards over the feet as you can, out to the side, back (without touching the ground) and then to the other side.

❸ Repeat five times, then reverse the circular movement and repeat another five times.

reverse bow   *This tones the spinal nerves and relieves tension and backache.*

❶ Lie down on your back and relax for a moment. Bend your knees, feet flat on the ground behind your buttocks, and put your hands beside your buttocks, elbows tucked in.

❷ On an in breath, lift your back off the floor, as high as you can, and support it with your hands. Your back will arch so that you are resting on your neck, shoulders, upper arms and feet. Keep breathing and stay in this posture for a few moments.

❸ Gently come back down, placing your hands flat on the floor beside you.

❹ Repeat twice more if you want. Then stretch out on the floor, take a deep breath and relax for a moment.

Now prepare yourself for Inner Conscious Relaxation.

4

inner conscious relaxation (20–25 minutes)

Find a comfortable position lying down. Take a deep breath and blow it out. Relax your body by bringing awareness to your toes and working your way up, releasing tension in the feet ... legs ... back of the body ... chest ... hands ... arms ... shoulders ... neck ... head. Repeat silently to yourself, 'I am aware I am practising Inner Conscious Relaxation'. Watch incoming and outgoing breath, breathing naturally, for a few moments. Now create your resolve, the statement or affirmation concerning your life that is inspiring or meaningful to you. Use the affirmation suggested on page 107 if you wish. Repeat this three times. At the end of the practice when you read or hear the words 'Peace ... Peace ... Peace', repeat your resolve three more times.

Now systematically rotate your consciousness through your body. As you mentally focus on each part of the body, name it silently and also try to visualize that part in your mind. Go slowly.

Right hand thumb ... second finger ... third finger ... fourth finger ... fifth finger ... palm ... wrist ... lower arm ... elbow ... upper arm ... shoulder ... armpit ... waist ... hip ... thigh ... knee ... calf ... ankle ... heel ... sole ... ball of the right foot ... the big toe ... second ... third ... fourth ... fifth toe ... left hand thumb ... second finger ... third ... fourth ... fifth ... palm ... wrist ... lower arm ... elbow ... upper arm ... shoulder ... armpit ... waist ... hip ... thigh ... knee ... calf ... ankle ... heel ... sole ... ball of the left foot ... the big toe ... second ... third ... fourth ... fifth toe ... right shoulder blade ... left shoulder blade ... spinal cord ... the whole of the back ... left buttock ... right buttock ... genitals ... pelvis ... stomach ... navel ... right chest ... left chest ... centre of the chest ... neck ... chin ... upper lip ... lower lip ... both lips together ... nose ... nose tip ... right cheek ... left cheek ... right temple ... left temple ... right ear ... left ear ... right eye ... left eye ... right eyelid ... left eyelid ... right eyebrow ... left eyebrow ... centre of the eyebrows ... forehead ... top of the head ... back of the head ... whole body ... awareness of the whole body.

toe ... calf ... knee ... thigh ... hip ... waist ... armpit ... shoulder ... upper arm ... elbow ... lower arm ...

Maintain awareness of your breathing for a few moments. Now let your mind scan your body. Become aware of any sensations, pleasant or unpleasant. Do these change, or are they constant? Continue to scan, simply observing without any judgement. Stay with this for a few moments.

Now focus on the heartspace, in the centre of your chest, and breathe into it. The heart is the source of unconditional love that supports your whole being. With each breath feel your heartspace opening out and let that love embrace you.

Now visualize yourself on a beautiful golden sandy beach, the waves lapping at your feet. You feel completely at ease. Ahead you see a fire burning and people sitting around it, making offerings of herbs. A holy woman is with them ... she is leading them in chanting Om. There is a feeling of great happiness in your heart.

As you come closer you see that the people are your friends, people you have always known and loved. The holy woman appears like a goddess ... radiant ... luminous ... as you sit together there is a deep joy ... a realization that you are loved totally and completely and that all beings and creatures are your friends ... that in essence there is no separation, only the one pure light that illuminates all hearts.

Unconditional happiness fills your heart. Feel it as connected to universal love, to that which supports the whole universe. This universal love nourishes you, you become one with it. Know that your life is a gift to be cherished. Feel the peace and the joy of this love.

Peace ... Peace ... Peace. Become aware of the resolve that you made at the beginning of the practice, and repeat it three times to yourself.

Now watch your breathing for a few moments ... move your fingers and toes ... externalize your consciousness. The practice of ICR is over. When you are ready, slowly roll over on to your side, then gently sit up. Have a smile on your face.

... fingers ... neck ... chin ... lips ... nose ... cheek ... temple ... ear ... eyebrow ... forehead ... top of head

4

dancing (10 minutes)

This exercise is simple. Just make sure that you will not be disturbed, put on your favourite music – and dance! If you do not have any particular music you feel that you can move to, then we suggest African drumming or tribal music, which has wonderful rhythms. Let your body leap, twist, spin, turn and bend to the beat. Dance your feelings, dance your relationships, dance your health and your joy. Let yourself go completely into the music so that your body dances you. As you move your body, feel it loosening and releasing; let it be free. Remember to breathe. When you have finished, simply stand or lie down for a few minutes as your heart slows down, and enjoy the sensation of energy in your body.

loving kindness
meditation (25 minutes)

The aim of this meditation is to develop a deeper experience of unconditional love and kindness. We start by developing it for ourselves, then slowly extend it to embrace our family and loved ones, then to those with whom we may be in conflict, and then towards all beings. In this way we go beyond thinking about being loving to actually experiencing it in our hearts. Developing loving kindness is not always easy, especially if we have been hurt. Here you are asked to transform your fear into compassion, bringing you more deeply into the love within yourself. This teaches us that all beings are equal and worthy of being loved – including you.

the practice Find a comfortable sitting position, and take a deep breath as you settle your body. Now bring your attention to your breath and to the heart-space – the area in the centre of your chest – and breathe into it. Begin to visualize in your heart an image of yourself, or repeat your name, or simply feel your presence there. Hold yourself in your heart as a mother would hold a child – gently and tenderly. Silently repeat to yourself, 'May I be well, may I be happy, may I be filled with loving kindness.' Keep repeating these words in your heart. As you do this, acknowledge any opposing thoughts that might arise – reasons why you should not be happy or well, feelings of guilt or shame, or of not being worthy of love. Acknowledge these and let them go. Continue repeating, 'May I be well, may I be happy, may I be filled with loving kindness.' Breathe in loving kindness, breathe out any tension. Embrace yourself, wish yourself health, happiness and peace; accept, appreciate and love yourself completely as you are. Stay with this for a few minutes.

Now bring into your heart those people you love or who are most important to you. (If you wish, you can focus on just one person each time you practise.) Begin with your family, then your friends, visualizing them or repeating their names. Share your love with these precious beings. Silently repeat, 'May you be well, may you be happy, may you be filled with loving kindness.' See how you are connected to each other, appreciating the beauty that each person has to offer. Breathing into your heart, release any difficulties that there may have been between you, any differences of opinion. You can also bring into your heart any past teachers or mentors or those who have guided you. Offer them your loving kindness and the common thread of humanity that links us all. Stay with this for a few minutes.

Now feel your heart reaching out towards someone with whom you are in conflict. Bring this person into your heart and expand your loving kindness and compassion towards them. Let your acceptance, love and forgiveness flow towards this person. Silently repeat, 'May you be well, may you be happy, may you be filled with loving kindness.' Breathe out any tension, and let the love in your heart reach out to them. Pain, hurt and anger are born when we close our hearts to each other, forgeting that we are all interconnected. Open your heart now, releasing the differences between you and reaching deeper into your love. Stay with this for a few minutes.

Now, slowly let your love radiate outwards, like the **ripples on a pond**, reaching out to all beings in all directions. Your heart opens to all beings everywhere, whoever they may be. 'May all beings be well, may all beings be happy, may all beings be filled with loving kindness.'

Seek out any prejudices you may hold and let them go. Every being is worthy of your love, whoever they are. Feel your relatedness to all beings, for ultimately we are all one. 'May all beings be at peace and may I be at peace with all beings.'

After a few minutes bring your awareness back to yourself in your heart. Know that the more love you give to others, the more will fill your being, just as the flame of a candle can light a thousand others without losing its own flame. This love knows no barriers, no limitations; it goes beyond all conditions.

As you gently come out of this meditation, feel that love filling you with joy and bringing a smile to your lips. May all beings be at peace.

4 lifestyle changes

diet Step 4 is about developing loving kindness towards ourselves and our world, so throughout this step see how much you can put this into practice in your diet and lifestyle. Try being a vegetarian throughout this time, or at least for one or two days a week. If you are already a vegetarian, then explore other areas in your diet where you can be kinder, more appreciative and do less harm to yourself or your world. Consider substituting soya milk products for dairy foods, clearing up the rubbish in your local park, or only buying foods that guarantee workers' rights.

Being kind to ourselves in our diet does not necessarily mean treating ourselves to a slice of chocolate cake. It may actually require us to eat less sugar, less fat, and less of those things that are not so nutritious. Be kind to your digestion by giving it gentle and nourishing foods; be kind to your heart and liver by eating less rich food, and be kind to your whole body by exercising more and by practising deep breathing. Honour your body's needs. Treat yourself to a massage or a sauna at least once a week, and take time to play and get more rest.

attitude Let your attitude for Step 4 be one of finding ways of practising kindness and generosity. Watch your feelings as you give, and observe if there is fear, trepidation or the need for acknowledgement within you. You do not need acclaim in order to give. Perhaps you can volunteer to help a local charity, offer to be a hospital visitor, visit the elderly or a children's home, or spend an evening serving food to the homeless. Practise random acts of kindness, such as putting money in someone's empty parking meter or carrying someone's shopping. Each day find one kind act to do and watch how it makes you feel. See your life fill with beauty and share that beauty with those around you. At the end of this step notice how much your attitude to kindness has changed.

anytime loving kindness

This exercise shows you how you can put loving kindness into practice at all times, not just when you are meditating. It is amazing the effect it can have, both on you and others, even though they do not know what you are doing.

As you go through your day, silently repeat, 'May you be well' or, 'May you be happy' to each person you see. Try doing this for one whole day, or for longer if you can. It is important not to tell anyone – just feel it in your heart. Do this wherever you are and to whomever you are with. For instance, repeat, 'May all things go well for you' if your boss shouts at you, 'May you be happy' when your partner is upset with you, or 'May you be well' when a passing motorist refuses to give way.

Be aware of the feelings that arise in you as you do this and to whom you find it the hardest to send good wishes. Watch how difficult it is for you, but keep going and your good wishes will soon become real feelings.

5

healing the
inner wounds

To be healed means to become whole. This is quite different from being cured, which is simply to fix a particular part. We can remove a stressor, but this will only provide temporary relief if we do not also address our tendency to become stressed. In order to heal stress we have to heal ourselves, so that our entire being is brought into a state of wholeness. This means bringing awareness to those parts of ourselves that have not been recognized, completed or resolved, and where feelings are being repressed, denied or ignored. Wherever there is repression, we are not whole. For instance, if we carry long-term resentment or grievance against someone, this can pervade every aspect of ourselves. We may get angry or irritated more quickly, be less able to love unconditionally, or we may feel that we are somehow wrong or bad, all of which contribute greatly to our stress levels. Even if we go on holiday and try to relax, or remove the external causes of our stress, the unexpressed parts of us remain tense.

Healing occurs in the present, not the past. We are not held back by the love we didn't receive in the past, but by the love we're not extending in the present.

MARIANNE WILLIAMSON

Step 5 is about healing our inner wounds so that we can enter into a deeper state of wholeness. This means taking time to discover the nature of the difficulties that are affecting us, and then finding the courage to face them. To do this takes great love and compassion for ourselves. We must look at ourselves with great honesty: at our addictions, habits, negative attitudes and repressed issues. Where are you holding on to old pain? Where are you denying your real feelings? What needs to be acknowledged, embraced or released? Does something need to be voiced? How can you bring your will and personal power into force to lift yourself out of suffering and into awareness and

Each morning we are born again. What we do today is what matters most. THE BUDDHA

acceptance? These issues are the concern of the throat chakra, where purification and healing find expression.

Healing is often synonymous with forgiveness, for a lack of forgiveness eats away at us, causing untold suffering, not least the desire for revenge. Forgiveness benefits us more than anyone else, certainly more than the other person who we believe to be at fault, for it is within ourselves that the pain is greatest and the healing most needed. Forgiveness releases that pain, leaving us free to love again, to give, care and trust. We are free to sing our own song. In forgiving another, we let go of the power they hold over us and regain our dignity and self-worth.

I bring **healing** and **forgiveness** to my inner wounds, and **release all** limitations to the **expression** of my heart through my voice and my actions.

To forgive does not mean we dismiss what has happened. By forgiving we are not condoning the act, for that may well be completely unacceptable – but we can forgive the person. We are not forgiving the transgressor for what occurred, but we are exonerating that person of not knowing how to be kind, of not having an open heart, or of being so overwhelmed by their own feelings that they could not see our own. We can do this because we can recognize those same stumbling blocks in ourselves – those places where we get lost in our own feelings to the exclusion of everyone else, or where we are so fraught or upset that anything that gets in our way suffers. We therefore need to forgive ourselves as much as we need to forgive another. Step 5 includes the release of our inner wounds to heal the present, and an opening of the depth of love that is within us. When our heart speaks, love finds its voice.

The beginning of the path of healing is the end of life unlived.

STEPHEN LEVINE

5

tree dance (15 minutes)

Find a piece of music you really like that has a medium tempo. If you want, you can try this with a different piece of music each morning. In this dance, you stay rooted until the climax as your body awakens from your head down to your feet.

Begin by standing with your legs about a foot apart, so that you feel grounded and balanced. Then start to move your head, gently, in all directions, loosening your jaw, facial muscles and neck. Feel as if you are a tree and the wind is stirring the top branches. Let your neck and head roll and let go, while keeping the rest of your body still.

As the wind begins to pick up, your upper body slowly begins to move: lift and move your shoulders in ways you have never moved them before, up and down, back and forth. Now move your fingers, hands, wrists, elbows and arms, stretching and bending in all directions.

Begin to move your rib cage and upper back, opening and releasing. Bend and release the whole of your body above your waist.

The wind is picking up more now as you move your hips and the whole of your back, swaying and bending in all directions. Feel your spine opening and releasing, move your hips round and back and forwards.

Now add your thighs and knees, while still keeping your feet rooted to the ground. The whole of your body is swaying and bending in the wind. Bend your knees, releasing the tension in your legs while your feet stay still.

Then the wind gets so strong that the tree is uprooted and is free to bend and dance and move wherever it wants to. Free your ankles, feet and toes to dance. Let your body dance you, as wild as the wild wind, as free as a soaring bird. Dance as long as you want to.

As the wind gently subsides, your tree begins to put its roots back into the ground. Slowly come back to the centre. Finally, just stand absolutely still with your eyes closed and breathe into that stillness.

inner conscious relaxation (20–25 minutes)

Find a comfortable position lying down. Take a deep breath and blow it out. Relax your body by bringing awareness to your toes and working your way up, releasing tension in the feet ... legs ... back of the body ... chest ... hands ... arms ... shoulders ... neck ... head. Repeat silently to yourself, 'I am aware I am practising Inner Conscious Relaxation'. Watch incoming and outgoing breath, breathing naturally, for a few moments. Now create your resolve, the statement or affirmation concerning your life that is inspiring or meaningful to you. Use the affirmation suggested on page 119 if you wish. Repeat this three times. At the end of the practice when you read or hear the words 'Peace ... Peace ... Peace', repeat your resolve three more times.

Now systematically rotate your consciousness through your body. As you mentally focus on each part of the body, name it silently and also try to visualize that part in your mind. Go slowly.

Right hand thumb ... second finger ... third finger ... fourth finger ... fifth finger ... palm ... wrist ... lower arm ... elbow ... upper arm ... shoulder ... armpit ... waist ... hip ... thigh ... knee ... calf ... ankle ... heel ... sole ... ball of the right foot ... the big toe ... second ... third ... fourth ... fifth toe ... left hand thumb ... second finger ... third ... fourth ... fifth ... palm ... wrist ... lower arm ... elbow ... upper arm ... shoulder ... armpit ... waist ... hip ... thigh ... knee ... calf ... ankle ... heel ... sole ... ball of the left foot ... the big toe ... second ... third ... fourth ... fifth toe ... right shoulder blade ... left shoulder blade ... spinal cord ... the whole of the back ... left buttock ... right buttock ... genitals ... pelvis ... stomach ... navel ... right chest ... left chest ... centre of the chest ... neck ... chin ... upper lip ... lower lip ... both lips together ... nose ... nose tip ... right cheek ... left cheek ... right temple ... left temple ... right ear ... left ear ... right eye ... left eye ... right eyelid ... left eyelid ... right eyebrow ... left eyebrow ... centre of the eyebrows ... forehead ... top of the head ... back of the head ... whole body ... awareness of the whole body.

toe ... calf ... knee ... thigh ... hip ... waist ... armpit ... shoulder ... upper arm ... elbow ... lower arm ...

Maintain awareness of your breathing for a few moments. Now bring your awareness to your nostrils. Mentally breathe in through your left nostril, breathe out through your right nostril and count one; breathe in through the right nostril and out through the left, count two; breathe in through the left, out through the right, three; breathe in through the right nostril and out through the left, four; then breathe in and out through both nostrils, five. That makes one round. Continue like this for three rounds. Then take a deep breath.

Now visualize yourself walking down a country lane. The air is laden with the scent of wild flowers, the birds are singing. You come to a small path leading across fields and, carefree as a child, you play there amongst the tall grasses. The path leads to a beautiful old wood ... you feel safe and welcome here. In the centre is a glade filled with streaming sunlight. As you walk towards it, you feel revitalized, your anxieties dropping away. Entering the glade you feel you are in a special, sacred place.

From the far side of the glade you see a figure coming towards you: a gentle, loving being, there to bring you healing. Together you sit in the glade. The healer lays gentle, caring hands on you and you feel a healing purity pouring through your whole being. All stress is removed. The healer offers you advice and words of self-renewal. You stay together for a few minutes.

Then slowly the figure leaves the glade. You feel deep gratitude in your heart. As you walk from the glade your footsteps are light, your body is vibrant and joyful.

Peace ... Peace ... Peace. Become aware of the resolve that you made at the beginning of the practice, and repeat it three times to yourself.

Now watch your breathing for a few moments ... move your fingers and toes ... externalize your consciousness. The practice of ICR is over. When you are ready, slowly roll over on to your side, then gently sit up. Have a smile on your face.

... fingers ... neck ... chin ... lips ... nose ... cheek ... temple ... ear ... eyebrow ... forehead ... top of head

breathe and move (10 minute

standing breath *Combining movement with the breath has a profoundly relaxing and releasing effect. This exercise balances the entire body. Go slowly and with awareness.*

1 Stand with your feet slightly apart and parallel, hands by your sides, with the palms facing forwards. Eyes are gently lowered. As you breathe in, lift your hands to meet at chest level in the prayer position; as you breathe out, gently move your hands back to your sides. Repeat twice more, moving with the breath.

2 On the next in breath, bring your hands to the prayer position, then take them on up and stretch them above your head, keeping your palms pressed together; on the out breath, bring them back to the chest, then down to your sides. Repeat twice more.

3 On the next in breath, take your hands to the prayer position, then all the way up above your head as before; hold them there for a moment. On the out breath, stretch your arms all the way out to the sides, then bring them down again. Repeat twice more.

4 On the next in breath, have your palms facing forward and stretch your arms out to the sides. Bring your palms together above your head, reversing the previous posture. Hold for a moment, then on the out breath bring your hands back to the prayer position and down to your sides. Repeat twice more. When you have finished, stand and relax for a few moments, just breathing.

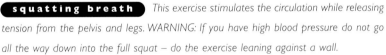

squatting breath *This exercise stimulates the circulation while releasing tension from the pelvis and legs. WARNING: If you have high blood pressure do not go all the way down into the full squat – do the exercise leaning against a wall.*

1 Stand with your feet fairly wide apart. Lift your arms above your head and cross your hands, right over left.

2 Breathe in and, stretching your arms out to the sides as you lower your body, go down into a gentle squat (only as far as is comfortable), bringing your arms down with the hands together at your heart, left over right. Bend your head forwards. Take a deep breath then, lifting the arms out to the sides, rise up to an upright standing position again, bringing your arms above your head, hands crossed right over left. Continue for five more rounds. When you have finished, stand with your hands by your sides as you breathe and relax.

side stretch *This exercise opens your chest and upper body while releasing the spine.*

1 Stand with your feet a foot apart and stretch your arms up over your head. Then clasp your elbows so that your arms are folded above your head, your right hand on your left elbow, your left hand on your right elbow.

2 On an out breath, bend from the waist as far as you can to the right, keeping your torso as straight as possible and without moving the hips; on an in breath come back up to the centre.

3 On the next out breath, bend all the way to the left, and on the in breath come back up. Repeat three to five times on each side. Then lower your arms and stand still for a moment. Now give yourself a good shake all over, and take a deep breath.

forgiveness

meditation (25 minutes)

Past pain, blame and shame imprison us, while forgiveness releases their hold, freeing us to love and receive again. It is important that you are ready to forgive – that you acknowledge the hurt, anger and sense of injustice – so that you do not repress any feelings and can move forward. Remember that you are not forgiving the act, rather the ignorance that allowed such behaviour. This meditation is essential for releasing the layers of inner pain that stop us from being healed.

In this practice, you start by finding forgiveness for yourself, opening your heart to the depth of feeling that is there and embracing it with love and acceptance. When we can forgive ourselves, we can then bring that forgiveness to another. The other person does not have to know anything about this; the important thing is that the forgiveness is in our own hearts.

the practice Find a comfortable sitting position. Bring your awareness to the breath as it enters and leaves your body as you settle, then begin to focus on your heartspace, the area in the centre of your chest. Breathe out any tension or stress, and with each in breath feel quietness and openness expanding.

Bring an image or thought of yourself into that area. Visualize and hold yourself there, with gentleness. As you do so, become aware of forgiveness and open up to forgiving yourself. Silently and slowly repeat, 'I forgive myself. I forgive myself for any harm I have done, for any pain I have caused, whether through my words or my actions. I forgive myself.'

Keep repeating these words. As you do so, all sorts of resistances may arise, all the reasons why you should not be forgiven, the things that you have done that are unworthy, and the shame or guilt associated with these. Breathe into these memories and resistances, acknowledge them and let them go. It is important to continue repeating the words and generating forgiveness. Release the resistances with your out breath; come back to forgiveness with your in breath.

Let forgiveness fill your entire being. Hold yourself in your heart as a mother holds her child, tenderly, with complete acceptance. Keep repeating, 'I forgive myself.' Stay with this for a few minutes.

Now bring into your heart someone who needs to be forgiven by you, someone whom you would like to forgive. Hold this person in your heart. Breathe into any feelings that arise; breathe out any anger, pain or fear, and breathe in forgiveness. Soften your belly, let go of resistance. Silently repeat, 'I forgive you. I forgive you. For the harm you have inflicted and the pain you have caused, through your words and your actions, I forgive you.'

This meditation may not be easy at first, but each step leads towards deeper healing. Take your time, keep repeating the words. Recognize your pain and let it go. Breathe out all the reasons why this person should not be forgiven – all the times or ways that they have hurt you – and breathe in forgiveness. Hold this person in your heart, feel your forgiveness embracing them. Silently repeat, 'I forgive you.' Stay with this for a few minutes.

Now bring into your heart someone you may have wronged, who has been hurt by you. Hold them in your heart with love and forgiveness. Silently repeat the words, 'I ask for your forgiveness. I ask for your forgiveness. If I have hurt you or caused you pain, through my words or my actions, please forgive me.'

Breathe into any resistance you may feel, any resentment and hurt. Accept your own ignorance, your own humility and mistakes. Breathe out resistance and breathe in forgiveness. Keep repeating the words. Feel your heart opening to forgiveness. Know that you are forgiven, that forgiveness is being given to you. Repeat, 'I am forgiven, I am forgiven.' Stay with this for a few minutes.

Now come back to yourself in your heart. Feel the joy of forgiveness in every part of your being. You are forgiven. You have forgiven. You have been forgiven. Let the release and the gratitude pour through you. Let the love that is within you radiate throughout your entire being. Rejoice in the forgiveness!

May all beings live in love. Take a deep breath and greet your world.

lifestyle changes

diet This is a time for purification and cleansing. By now you will be better in tune with your own dietary needs, so vary the following suggestions to suit yourself and your lifestyle. Try having nothing but fruit and fruit juice until midday each day. Eat as much as you want of as many different fruits as you like. This will help to cleanse and revitalize your system. For lunch (or the evening meal if lunch is your main meal) have a large bowl of mixed salad, as many raw vegetables as possible, and cooked whole grains, such as brown rice. For your main meal, focus on baked or steamed foods: baked carrots, parsnips, potatoes, onions, tofu or fish, and steamed green vegetables. Drink only herb teas but plenty of them. Try to avoid fats, dairy foods, meat, refined foods, fried foods, sugar, caffeine and stimulants. If this is too much for you to do every day, then attempt it at least twice a week. It will stimulate your system and help to eliminate toxins, releasing energy and healing.

attitude Now is the time to become clear and honest in your speech, to apply awareness to what you say and the effect it has on others. Observe how you use your language to manipulate and control others, or to hide what you are really feeling. Try to use your voice only for true expression, to speak your feelings, and to express your care and love. This is an opportunity to purify your speech and to give your heart full expression.

Sing more – let your throat open and your voice soar. If you are shy of singing, try taking some lessons to gain greater confidence. Discover the lost parts of you and put sounds to them. Let your feelings sing. Sing to the wind or the sun, sing to your parents, your lover, your past. And, most definitely, sing in the bath!

This is an exercise to help you to see where mental and emotional healing is needed. Consider what issues in your life are incomplete or unresolved. There may be an issue from the past that you have never been able to forget or forgive, or a recent difficulty that has caused conflict. Choose just one problem to work with at any one time.

Begin by writing down everything that you can think of that, from your point of view, applies to this issue. Be clear about your feelings, your reasons, your injustices or hurts. Describe how you were treated, how you felt, if you were ignored, if the behaviour towards you was disrespectful or dismissive. Then look at how you dealt with the situation. Did you express your feelings? Were you honest about what you were feeling? Or did you swallow what you really wanted to say? Spend as much time as you need to on this part of the exercise.

Then take a deep breath and pause before you consider the ways you treated the other person or people involved. Begin to write these down. What did you do to them? How do you think you made them feel? Did you listen to their arguments or feelings? Did you take these into account? Did you treat them with respect and dignity? Did you encourage them to say what they meant? Did you turn away from them?

Then take a moment to see if you can imagine what it might be like to be the other person. Can you look at the issue from their point of view? Can you feel their pain, confusion, ignorance? Can you feel their unexpressed feelings? Stay with this as long as you need to.

Take a deep breath. What insights have you gained from this exercise? Can you see where greater honesty, expression or healing might be needed? Is there something yet to be forgiven? This exercise is not to judge what you find but to deepen your awareness of the whole picture.

intuitive wisdom

Having opened our hearts, we now come to expanding our minds. Step 6 is about opening ourselves to a more profound level of perception so that we can discover our own truths and develop a deeper trust and respect for our insights, intuition and inner wisdom. We cannot access these qualities if we routinely make the insights of others more valid or important than our own, dismiss our observations as unworthy or meaningless, or, conversely, judge others' perceptions as wrong or invalid. Nor is it possible to know our own truth if we operate from false or ego-centred ideas, where fear or greed are the motivating forces behind our decisions or attitudes.

It is vital that we see where we hold prejudices or are closed to another's view. It is natural to believe that the way we see things is the only way, or at least the right way. It is not so easy to admit that someone else's viewpoint might be equally valid. Look at these letters and read out what they spell:

Don't believe what your eyes are telling you. All they show is limitation. Look with your understanding, find out what you already know, and you'll see the way to fly.

RICHARD BACH

THEPOTENTIALISNOWHERE

Some people will arrange the letters into the words 'the potential is nowhere', while others will interpret them as 'the potential is now here'. There is a huge difference between these two meanings, yet it rests simply on how we look at things, on our beliefs and attitudes. It shows us that there is truth in every viewpoint, not just our own: as much as you see something one way, someone else will see it differently, and you both are right.

The power of the mind is enormous. The more we limit ourselves — by blaming others for our mental anguish, maintaining rigid beliefs, prejudices or attitudes, resisting change or new ideas, or by holding negative attitudes while pretending everything is fine — the further we will be from our truth

Our own worst enemy cannot harm us as much as our unwise thoughts. No one can help as much as our own compassionate thoughts. THE BUDDHA

and from inner peace. Only when we see ourselves with complete honesty, recognizing the ways in which we restrict our minds and prevent ourselves from knowing our truth, will we be able to go deeper and discover the insights that have always been there, waiting to be uncovered.

In this step we will work on developing the third eye chakra, located at the brow. It is the third eye that penetrates through delusion, sees clearly the bigger picture, not just our own small one, and through that vision is able to reach our

I bring insight and intuition to every situation and trust my innate wisdom.

innate wisdom. This is not the same as developing the intellect; rather, it is the ability to realize spiritual truths that perceive the deeper levels of human existence.

As a man thinketh, so he will be.

THE BIBLE

To embark on this journey, we need, above all, time to ourselves in which to reflect. When we create a space and enter into the quietness, we can hear our inner wisdom speak. It is natural to feel doubts, to wonder if our insights are really worth anything, but we need to trust what we hear. Having faith in our intuition is essential if we are to live in wisdom. Try reflecting on a past incident or situation and see if you can get in touch with what you were really feeling at the time. In retrospect, can you recognize the wisdom in your thoughts? Or take a current circumstance that feels to you like a hindrance, an irritation, or even a disaster, and attempt to penetrate it

There is no need to run outside
For better seeing,
Nor to peer from a window. Rather abide
At the centre of your being;
For the more you leave it, the less you learn.
Search your heart and see
If he is wise who takes each turn;
The way to do is to be.

LAO TZU

more deeply to find the truth within it. What is there for you to learn? What insights can you gain, either about yourself or others? How can you grow from this situation? Apply wisdom to an annoyance and watch it become a blessing – it just depends on your perspective and perception!

intuitive wisdom

stretching (15 minutes)

Spend a few moments stretching your whole body: stretch up on your toes, bend down to the floor, then stand up and shake and loosen your arms and legs.

moon pose *This posture relaxes the lower spinal nerves and opens the pelvis.*

❶ Kneel on the floor with your buttocks resting on your heels. Stretch your arms up over your head, pointing your hands to the sky, with the palms facing forwards.

❷ Take a deep breath and on the out breath bend forwards until your hands and forehead touch the floor. Stretch your hands out in front of you as far as you can, keeping your buttocks close to your heels. Take a breath.

❸ On the next inhalation, stretch upwards to the sky again. Repeat twice more.

cat pose *This posture is excellent for spinal flexibility, releasing all stiffness.*

❶ Kneel on all fours, with your knees hip-distance apart and your hands flat on the floor under your shoulders, like a cat.

❷ On an inhalation, arch the spine downwards so that your back is concave, and raise your head.

❸ On an exhalation, arch the spine upwards and lower the head.

❹ Continue this movement, remembering to keep your arms straight and your weight evenly distributed. Feel like a cat stretching your back. Enjoy the rhythm of the movement for at least ten rounds, breathing deeply. Then sit back on your heels in Moon Pose (2) and relax for a moment.

cobra and triangle pose *This is an extension of Cat Pose, adding extra movement and ease to the spine and abdomen. WARNING: Do not do this exercise if you have high blood pressure.*

❶ Stretch out on the floor on your front. Place your hands flat under your shoulders, elbows pointing up, forehead to the ground.

❷ On an in breath, push up on your hands and lift your torso and head up and back into Cobra Pose, keeping your elbows close to your body. Relax in this pose for one or two breaths.

❸ From here, tuck the toes under and, on an out breath, straighten your arms and lift your buttocks up into Triangle Pose, with your palms and feet flat on the ground. Relax your head and neck and feel the stretch in your leg muscles and back.

4 On an in breath, bend the elbows and lower your body back to the ground. Turn the toes over and lift the head and trunk upwards into Cobra Pose, keeping the elbows close to the body. This is one round.

5 Continue for another two rounds. Then stretch out on your back for a few moments, breathing gently and relaxing completely.

head rest *This pose is excellent for opening out the neck and chest.*

1 Sit upright with your legs straight out in front of you, and your hands on the floor by your thighs.

2 Lean backwards, slowly and gently, until you are almost lying down. Then tip your head back so that the top of it is resting on the ground and your back is arched upwards.

3 Take a few deep breaths in this position, then gently lift your head up, lower your back to the ground and relax.

rock and roll *This is a wonderful movement for opening and releasing the spine. Make sure you do this on a carpet, mat or folded blanket.*

1 Bring both your knees to your chest and clasp them with your hands.

2 First rock from side to side, massaging your lower spine and buttocks.

3 Then begin to rock gently forwards and backwards along your spine, increasing the movement as feels comfortable. Continue for a few minutes, taking care not to hurt your back.

4 Then stretch out, take a few deep breaths and relax for a few moments.

Now prepare yourself for Inner Conscious Relaxation.

inner **conscious relaxation** (25 minutes)

Find a comfortable position lying down. Take a deep breath and blow it out. Relax your body by bringing awareness to your toes and working your way up, releasing tension in the feet ... legs ... back of the body ... chest ... hands ... arms ... shoulders ... neck ... head. Repeat silently to yourself, 'I am aware I am practising Inner Conscious Relaxation'. Watch incoming and outgoing breath, breathing naturally, for a few moments. Now create your resolve, the statement or affirmation concerning your life that is inspiring or meaningful to you. Use the affirmation suggested on page 131 if you wish. Repeat this three times. At the end of the practice when you read or hear the words 'Peace ... Peace ... Peace', repeat your resolve three more times.

Now systematically rotate your consciousness through your body. As you mentally focus on each part of the body, name it silently and also try to visualize that part in your mind. Go slowly.

Right hand thumb ... second finger ... third finger ... fourth finger ... fifth finger ... palm ... wrist ... lower arm ... elbow ... upper arm ... shoulder ... armpit ... waist ... hip ... thigh ... knee ... calf ... ankle ... heel ... sole ... ball of the right foot ... the big toe ... second ... third ... fourth ... fifth toe ... left hand thumb ... second finger ... third ... fourth ... fifth ... palm ... wrist ... lower arm ... elbow ... upper arm ... shoulder ... armpit ... waist ... hip ... thigh ... knee ... calf ... ankle ... heel ... sole ... ball of the left foot ... the big toe ... second ... third ... fourth ... fifth toe ... right shoulder blade ... left shoulder blade ... spinal cord ... the whole of the back ... left buttock ... right buttock ... genitals ... pelvis ... stomach ... navel ... right chest ... left chest ... centre of the chest ... neck ... chin ... upper lip ... lower lip ... both lips together ... nose ... nose tip ... right cheek ... left cheek ... right temple ... left temple ... right ear ... left ear ... right eye ... left eye ... right eyelid ... left eyelid ... right eyebrow ... left eyebrow ... centre of the eyebrows ... forehead ... top of the head ... back of the head ... whole body ... awareness of the whole body.

toe ... calf ... knee ... thigh ... hip ... waist ... armpit ... shoulder ... upper arm ... elbow ... lower arm ...

Maintain awareness of your breathing for a few moments. Now become aware of the whole of your body and the contact point between your body and the ground. Scan from your feet all the way up to your head, focusing on that point of contact between your body and the ground. Then bring your awareness to your breathing. Follow each breath in and out. As you do this begin to intone SO with each in breath, and HUM with each out breath. In and out: So Hum. Let yourself sink into the rhythm of your breath and the mantra for a few minutes.

Now visualize that you are walking in a beautiful garden filled with wild birdsong. You feel like a young child here, safe and protected, free to explore and play.

After a while you see a figure coming towards you ... it is a holy man, a wise man, he is smiling with great tenderness and compassion ... you feel pure love emanating from him ... as he greets you, his peace is like a warm embrace, an unconditional acceptance ... you feel as if he knows you completely, that you are safe and protected. His wisdom fills you with understanding. You walk through the garden together, holding hands. Spend a few minutes together before he gently leaves and you sit quietly in the garden, your heart full of love.

Bring your visualization to the space between and just above your eyebrows, to your third eye, looking from within. In that space visualize a white light. It may start very small, just a speck of light, but as you breathe and focus, the light will grow. Stay with this for a few moments.

Peace ... Peace ... Peace. Become aware of the resolve that you made at the beginning of the practice, and repeat it three times to yourself.

Now watch your breathing for a few moments ... move your fingers and toes ... externalize your consciousness. The practice of ICR is over. When you are ready, slowly roll over on to your side, then gently sit up. Have a smile on your face.

... fingers ... neck ... chin ... lips ... nose ... cheek ... temple ... ear ... eyebrow ... forehead ... top of head

6 breathing (15 minutes)

Begin with five minutes of fast walking, focusing on short, sharp breathing while you walk. Walk inside or outside, energizing your body. When you are done, stand absolutely still for a moment and watch your body energy flow.

full breath *This shows us most clearly how our breathing affects our emotions. Find a quiet place to sit with a straight back.*

1 Start by breathing only into the upper part of your chest – just below your collar bone – and as you do this watch your emotions. The breath will be short and quick, and is usually accompanied by feelings of fear, panic or anxiety. People who are stressed may breathe here much of the time.

2 Next, breathe for a few moments into the area just below your heart, around your upper abdomen. This area usually feels calmer and safer, the breath is more normal, although for very tense people it may be difficult to breathe into this area.

3 Now see if you can breathe into your lower abdomen, about an inch below your navel. The breath will be long and deep; it usually feels very relaxed, calm and centred. If it is easier, you can do this lying on the floor, which will relax the diaphragm enough for you to be able to breath more deeply.

4 Now see if you can join up these three levels in one long breath. Start by breathing in at the top ... fill the middle ... and then the belly ... pause and then empty the belly ... middle ... and then the top. Do this three times.

5 Then reverse the breath by breathing into and filling the belly ... then the middle ... and then the top ... then empty the top ... the middle ... and then the belly. Do this three times and relax.

Spending a few minutes each day breathing through these three levels will help you to gain greater control over your breathing and to relax deeply.

sun breath *This breathing technique enables you to breathe deeply, releasing all the stress in your body. You can either kneel, using a cushion between your buttocks and your heels, or stand with your feet about a foot apart. The in breath is described in three stages, but is actually one long continuous breath. Get used to the positions first, then add the breathing.*

1 Begin with your hands by your sides. Breathe into your belly and, at the same time, stretch your arms out to your sides.

2 Breathe into the middle part of your chest as you bring your hands together in the prayer position at your heart.

3 Breathe into the upper part of your chest as you lift your hands all the way up over your head, with the fingers joined and pointing to the sky, and with your head back. Pause for a moment.

4 On the out breath, take your hands all the way out to the sides and back down, as if outlining the sun. Pause and take a natural breath.

5 Repeat the sequence three times, or more if you like. Do this exercise slowly and with awareness.

witness meditation

(25 minutes)

When we witness ourselves – simply noting our breath, thoughts, feelings and bodily sensations without judgment – we begin to go beneath the surface to a deeper level of awareness. As we do this, however, we may find ourselves getting distracted by various internal dramas or anxieties. The purpose of this meditation is to help us maintain an objective awareness both of ourselves and of the discursive mind.

As we enter the meditative state, it gives us a degree of spaciousness, as if we have stepped out of the woods and can now look back and see the trees. From this vantage point we can notice each tendency of the mind, and how the mind works. We see that each individual thought is not the whole of us, it is only a part that comes and goes, and that we are made up of many different parts.

the practice Find a comfortable seated position. Take a deep breath and spend a few moments developing appreciation and gratitude for your environment and your breath. Bring your awareness to your body. Let your mind move through your body, witnessing and observing each part, starting at your toes ... your feet ... witness your legs ... knees ... thighs. Bring that awareness to your buttocks ... lower back ... middle back ... and upper back. Witness the whole of your back. Then observe your pelvis ... abdomen ... chest. Take a deep breath and witness how your body moves with the breath. Then observe your fingers ... hands ... arms ... elbows ... shoulders. Witness your neck ... jaw ... mouth ... nose ... eyes ... ears ... forehead ... and the back of your head. Simple and complete awareness of yourself as you are.

Now become aware of the natural flow of the breath ... witness the breath in all its detail. Watch where it comes into your body, the movement of the body and where the breath goes and how it leaves. Watch how the body feels as the breath moves through it. Watch the moments between each of the breaths. Stay with this for a few minutes.

Now become aware of your thoughts and witness them ... just let them arise spontaneously, whatever they are. Whether they are good or bad does not matter, just be an objective on-looker. Do not get involved, but maintain the observation ... see how your thoughts are like pictures on a screen. Watch your feelings arise. Notice if they have an effect on your body. Notice if one thought or feeling leads to another. Be a witness to yourself.

Now externalize your awareness. Become like a radar and send your awareness outside of yourself ... into the room you are in ... then out into the street ... further and further ... until it is a mile in radius. Become aware of all the sounds, but do not identify with any one ... just witness the sounds of life. Stay with this for a few minutes. Become as acutely aware as you can, observing whatever you hear without judgement. Keep going outwards.

Maintain awareness of your thoughts, simply watch how they come and go, how they create dramas and scenarios in your mind. Do not make the thoughts either good or bad, do not make yourself bad for having them – you are just an impartial observer of your thoughts.

Now bring your awareness inwards and become aware of the breath in your nostrils ... feel as if you are in there, watching the breath from the tip of your nose to the space between your eyebrows ... get closer and closer to the breath. Become aware of the eyebrow centre, just above and between your eyebrows, and see a tiny dot of light ... keep the gaze steady and absolutely focused ... watch the tiny dot expanding ... let the whole of your being be filled with light. This is the light of wisdom. Stay with this light for a few minutes.

Take a few moments to become aware of your breathing, your body and the room around you. Take a deep breath and have a good stretch, gently coming out of meditation. You may like to dedicate the benefits of this practice to all beings or simply feel thanks.

lifestyle changes

diet The object of Step 6 is to allow our natural wisdom to emerge in our lives, and that includes our diet and lifestyle, too. If you asked everyone you met if they knew what they should be eating or doing, most of them would say yes, they know that they should be eating less fat, less meat, less salt, less sugar, more vegetables, fruit and whole grains; that smoking and too much drinking can be detrimental to health; and that they should be getting a few hours' exercise each week. Then ask them if they are doing any of this and the answer is maybe some of it, or no, or they do not have time.

Developing wisdom means getting to know our own body and honouring its needs. It means acting on something because we know it is right – not because we feel we ought to – as an expression of love for ourselves. We need to put our truth into action.

Spend this time listening to your body, listening to your body's wisdom, and respect what you hear. Listen to when and what your body really wants to eat. And watch yourself. If you eat a whole bar of chocolate be honest about how you feel afterwards, how your skin reacts, how your stomach feels. Watch and learn. Only you can judge what is right for you. Make friends and communicate with your body – once you have learned its language, you will discover that it has great wisdom.

attitude During this step focus on being able to discriminate between false beliefs, which arise from ego and delusion, and inner truth, which arises from your deepest place of awareness. While delusion will lead to further suffering, confusion or desire, inner truth will lead to greater peace of mind, harmony and joy. Be aware of what triggers the ego, what things delude you into believing them to be true, and give your inner understanding room to express itself.

journal writing

Keeping a journal makes us take time for ourselves to be quiet and reflective. It gives us a chance to uncover what are our deeper thoughts and feelings — ones that may be hidden, difficult to accept, or even difficult to find — and to look at a given situation from different perspectives. It also enables us to be more objective and to give a voice to our innermost being. This is an essential part of developing insight.

Use a special note pad or book for your journal. Before you start to write, just sit quietly and breathe. Let your mind reflect back on any situation where you feel you need greater insight. As you do this, specifically look for your innermost responses — for what was really going on rather than what appeared to happen. Or simply write about your day, your meetings with others, your thoughts, your work, your relationships, your attitudes. Be honest — nobody is going to see this but you! See if you can recognize where you were responding from fear, greed, selfishness, expectation or ego, where delusion took over from clarity. Keep going deeper. From where do these responses arise? What are your real fears? What are you really needing that you are not getting?

Keep reflecting on the nature of the issue you are writing about. What insights can you gain about yourself? What is needed to bring more truth into your daily life? How can you go deeper into a place of trust so that you can express your truth?

inner peace

It takes time to discover that place within ourselves which is always at peace no matter how stressful the circumstances around us. We must first move through layers of fear, doubt, habit and resistance, and we can only do this by being patient, by continually renewing our commitment, and by taking time to be quiet with ourselves in meditation. As we deepen our faith and spiritual awareness, so we increase our trust, both in ourselves and in our understanding.

To be spiritual does not mean that we have to join a monastery or perform complex rituals. In essence we are all spiritual beings — whether we are aware of it or not. We are all in relationship to the Divine, to what gives meaning to life and nourishes the soul. Deep inside we know that we are more than just our bodies, more than our daily kaleidoscope of thoughts and emotions. It is up to each one of us to decide how much we are willing to bring that spiritual awareness into our lives.

You only need one step in order to enter the Kingdom of God. Just one step. When you hear a bird, or when you see a star, or the eyes of a child, you can enter the Kingdom of Heaven right away. THICH NHAT HANH

Without doubt, the more we do so, the more peace we will find.

Step 7 is about entering into spiritual consciousness; this means that we seek a relationship with our highest potential, the essence of who we truly are. This is the area of the crown chakra, the place of peace. Spiritual consciousness is not an isolated state, for the depth of our spiritual awareness pervades our whole being, colouring our every thought and action. Connecting with our spiritual nature frees us from the pull of the worldly — from greed, selfishness, loneliness, fear, hatred and revenge — and enables us to get in touch with a deep source of inner strength. It is from this place

In the end these things matter most: How well did you love? How fully did you live? How deeply did you learn to let go? THE BUDDHA

that we can express generosity, faith, grace and compassion. We are able to go beyond our ego-centred views to seeing the interplay of connectedness between all things and the divine grace that is with us at all times. It takes us from identifying with the content into direct experience of the essence.

Such an expanded view requires both surrender and faith. Surrender is about surrendering our ego, letting go of our self-centredness so that we become aware of our relationship to all things. Faith gives purpose and depth; without it there is meaninglessness or emptiness to life. Faith arises from the complete confidence that we can respond to life with the trust that deep within all beings is the Divine — that we all have the Buddha within us, even if it is a sleeping Buddha yet to awaken.

I am open to the depth and beauty of the Divine and welcome it into every part of my being and my life.

Spirituality is not the same as religion, it does not entail following any particular path, philosophy or teaching. However, Step 7 does ask that you question your beliefs and feelings about the Divine, and explore the role of faith in your life. Do you normally keep such issues inside a church? Do you believe that there is a spiritual dimension in life? Does this make you feel fearful? Or can you touch that place inside yourself that goes beyond the mundane and the physical, a place that is alive to a higher energy?

When we honour our spiritual being, and give voice to our highest self, a wonderful thing happens – we discover that our lives are changed for the better. We find we are more deeply at peace, we care and love more, we argue or get upset less. And this affects everyone around us – it gives permission to others also to go beyond their limitations and to experience their inner beauty. The more we give a voice to the qualities of spirit – to love, compassion and truth, opening ourselves to the great mystery – the more it will awaken us to freedom.

It is a rare privilege to be born as a human being, as we happen to be; If we do not achieve enlightenment in this life, when do we expect to achieve it? ECHU

Discovering and establishing our spirituality is not the end of the Seven Step Programme so much as the beginning of our real journey, which is the emergence of our true nature. This is the most joyous and stress-free journey possible!

stretching (15 minutes)

morning salutation This is a whole body stretch which brings into one sequence many of the positions that you have already done in other steps. It may take you a while to learn, but once you have mastered it, do it as one continuous movement. You can repeat it as many times as you like in each session. It will benefit your entire body.

7

Before you start, spend a few moments stretching: stretch your arms up and over your head, stretch your legs out, loosen your spine, take a deep breath and feel your lungs expand.

❶ Start by kneeling on the floor, buttocks resting on your heels, arms by your sides. On an inhalation, lift your arms out to the sides and then up over your head, hands pointing upwards.

❷ On an exhalation, bend forward into Moon Pose (see page 133), stretching your arms as far forwards as you can. Put your hands flat on the floor, keeping your buttocks close to your knees.

❸ On an inhalation, move your body along the floor over your hands, and bend your torso upwards into Cobra Pose (see page 134).

❹ Tuck your toes under and, on an exhalation, lower your back and lift your buttocks into the air, as in Triangle Pose (see page 134).

❺ On an inhalation, bend your right leg and bring your foot between your hands, keeping the left leg stretched out behind you but lowering the knee to the floor. Lift the head back and gaze upwards.

❻ On an exhalation, bring the left leg forwards and place the left foot beside the right one. Straighten the legs and bend forwards, resting your hands on your legs or the ground beside your feet.

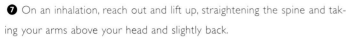

7 On an inhalation, reach out and lift up, straightening the spine and taking your arms above your head and slightly back.

8 On an exhalation, bend down again as before, hands as before on your legs or beside your feet.

9 On an inhalation, place your hands on the floor beside you and take your right foot straight back behind you, knee to the floor, and bend the left knee, the reverse of position 5.

10 On an exhalation, take the left foot back beside the right and lift your buttocks into Triangle Pose, as in position 4.

11 On an inhalation, lower your knees to the ground into Cat Pose (see page 133), lowering the spine into a downwards arch and lifting your head.

12 On an exhalation, lower your buttocks to sit on your heels, bring your forehead to the ground and relax your arms on the ground beside you. Take a deep breath. To begin the next round, inhale and lift up into the kneeling position (1), arms above your head.

When you have finished as many rounds as you like, stretch out on your back and relax completely.

Now prepare yourself for Inner Conscious Relaxation.

inner conscious relaxation (30 minutes)

Find a comfortable position lying down. Take a deep breath and blow it out. Relax your body by bringing awareness to your toes and working your way up, releasing tension in the feet ... legs ... back of the body ... chest ... hands ... arms ... shoulders ... neck ... head. Repeat silently to yourself, 'I am aware I am practising Inner Conscious Relaxation'. Watch incoming and outgoing breath, breathing naturally, for a few moments. Now create your resolve, the statement or affirmation concerning your life that is inspiring or meaningful to you. Use the affirmation suggested on page 145 if you wish. Repeat this three times. At the end of the practice when you read or hear the words 'Peace ... Peace ... Peace', repeat your resolve three more times.

Now systematically rotate your consciousness through your body. As you mentally focus on each part of the body, name it silently and also try to visualize that part in your mind. Go slowly.

Right hand thumb ... second finger ... third finger ... fourth finger ... fifth finger ... palm ... wrist ... lower arm ... elbow ... upper arm ... shoulder ... armpit ... waist ... hip ... thigh ... knee ... calf ... ankle ... heel ... sole ... ball of the right foot ... the big toe ... second ... third ... fourth ... fifth toe ... left hand thumb ... second finger ... third ... fourth ... fifth ... palm ... wrist ... lower arm ... elbow ... upper arm ... shoulder ... armpit ... waist ... hip ... thigh ... knee ... calf ... ankle ... heel ... sole ... ball of the left foot ... the big toe ... second ... third ... fourth ... fifth toe ... right shoulder blade ... left shoulder blade ... spinal cord ... the whole of the back ... left buttock ... right buttock ... genitals ... pelvis ... stomach ... navel ... right chest ... left chest ... centre of the chest ... neck ... chin ... upper lip ... lower lip ... both lips together ... nose ... nose tip ... right cheek ... left cheek ... right temple ... left temple ... right ear ... left ear ... right eye ... left eye ... right eyelid ... left eyelid ... right eyebrow ... left eyebrow ... centre of the eyebrows ... forehead ... top of the head ... back of the head ... whole body ... awareness of the whole body.

toe ... calf ... knee ... thigh ... hip ... waist ... armpit ... shoulder ... upper arm ... elbow ... lower arm ...

Maintain awareness of your breathing for a few moments. Now awaken the seven chakras by bringing the mind to the parts of the body that correspond to each chakra, visualizing a lotus and repeating the sound or mantra associated with it.

Bring your awareness to the root chakra located between the bladder and the anus. Focus your mind there and visualize a four-petalled deep red lotus flower and silently repeat the mantra LAM three times. Bring your awareness to the base chakra at the base of the spine and visualize a six-petalled orange lotus flower and mentally repeat the sound VAM three times. Now bring your awareness up the spine to the navel chakra at the point opposite the navel in the spine. Visualize a ten-petalled yellow lotus flower and silently repeat the mantra RAM three times. Now move your awareness to the heart chakra at the centre of the chest in the spinal region. Visualize a 12-petalled rose lotus flower and mentally repeat the sound YAM three times. Move up to the throat chakra in the throat area. Visualize a 16-petalled turquoise lotus and silently repeat the sound HAM three times. Now go to the third eye chakra at the centre of the eyebrows. Visualize a two-petalled violet lotus flower and mentally repeat the mantra OM three times. Now go to the top of the head to the crown chakra. Visualize a 1000-petalled rainbow-coloured lotus flower and repeat the sound OM three times.

Now move your mind up and down three times through these seven centres in sequence, repeating each sound vibration three times: root Lam; base Yam; navel Ram; heart Yam; throat Ham; third eye Om; crown Om. As you become more competent in this practice you can add the visualizations of the lotus flowers as you move up and down the chakras.

Peace ... Peace ... Peace. Become aware of the resolve that you made at the beginning of the practice, and repeat it three times to yourself.

Now watch your breathing for a few moments ... move your fingers and toes ... externalize your consciousness. The practice of ICR is over. When you are ready, slowly roll over on to your side, then gently sit up. Have a smile on your face.

... fingers ... neck ... chin ... lips ... nose ... cheek ... temple ... ear ... eyebrow ... forehead ... top of head

walking meditation (15 minutes)

The simple act of walking, like breathing, is usually done with little awareness. When we make it the focus of meditation, we discover that walking is a whole universe in itself. We are not trying to get anywhere, and we are not trying to do anything other than walk, slowly and mindfully. This is meditation in action, where the mind maintains a concentrated awareness while walking and pays attention to the movement at the same time.

You can walk slowly or quickly – all that matters is that you are walking with awareness. Walk indoors or outside. Walk along a beach or in a town park, in your garden or around your living room. Wear shoes or have bare feet. Walk in a large circle, or in a straight line, or back and forth between two points, perhaps about 30 paces apart.

Traditionally, Walking Meditation is alternated with Breath Awareness Meditation 1 or 2 (see pages 102–103 and 154–155) so that the body has a chance to move and re-energize between sitting sessions, but without losing concentration. You can do either of these practices first, whichever you prefer.

Start by standing up straight. Hold your left hand lightly in front of your abdomen in a closed position, with your right hand gently covering it so that it feels supported and comfortable. This position enables the arms to stay relaxed without tension in the shoulders. The eyes are kept open but looking down to only two to four feet in front; you need to see where you are going, to be aware of the world around you, but without being distracted or spending time looking about. If you want to do this practice outside, then have the eyes raised a little bit more so that you are aware of other people around you. In this way the practice becomes one of balancing the outer world with your inner world, with your feet acting as the bridge between the two.

the practice Begin to walk, being aware of how you lift, move and place each foot. As you walk silently repeat, 'lifting ... moving ... placing' with each step. You can move slowly, at a moderate pace, or a little faster if you need energizing. Your speed should synchronize with your concentration on the movement and the breath. Maintain awareness throughout, keeping your shoulders and neck relaxed, your movements completely flowing and your breathing natural.

When the mind becomes quiet and there is just walking, you will merge into the rhythm and beauty of the movement. If you are wearing shoes, be aware of how your feet feel and the meeting of the shoes with the ground; if you have bare feet, notice the texture and temperature of the ground, feel where it is bumpy or smooth, be aware of where your feet and the ground meet. If you are walking from one point to another, when you turn at each end of your path be aware of the change in movement and direction, and take a moment to shift your awareness as you walk ... stop ... turn ... then walk again.

When you have finished Walking Meditation, stand completely still for a few moments with your eyes closed, simply being aware of your breath and your body. Experience the stillness. Then open your eyes, take a deep breath, and slowly move back into your day, enjoying the sensation of movement.

breath awareness

meditation ~ 2 (30 minutes)

Find your normal meditation sitting posture. Settle yourself and spend a few moments appreciating your seat, the room around you, the earth beneath you, and your own body. Gently bring your appreciation to your breath, then become aware of the rhythm of each inhalation and exhalation. Bring your attention to where the breath enters and leaves the nostrils, or to the heartspace (the area in the centre of the chest), or to the area about an inch below the navel – whichever you find most comfortable. Just watch the breath from that place.

the practice Now, with each in breath, silently repeat, 'Breathing in', and with each out breath silently repeat, 'Breathing out'. If you prefer, you can simply repeat, 'In ... out' with each inhalation and exhalation. Continue like this for the duration of the meditation. As you do so, watch what happens. Be aware of your thoughts, of the distractions, and of the dramas that your mind creates. Just observe, let go, and come back to the breath as it moves in and out.

Breathing naturally, observe this process as it works by itself. Have no expectations, no desires of what might or might not happen. The more we try to meditate the less we will be still; the more we relax into just breathing, the quieter our minds will become. Just breathe one breath at a time, staying in the moment, coming back to the present whenever you drift.

Every so often check in with yourself and ask, 'Am I here now?', 'What are my thoughts in this moment?' Be aware of how you may have drifted into thought. Then continue watching the in and out flow.

There may be moments when you feel constrained or constricted by the breath, or you may find that you are breathing too quickly. If this happens, simply expand your awareness beyond yourself and witness whatever is going on around you or beyond the room. When you feel reorientated and balanced, come back to the breath, to the 'In ... out' rhythm. At other times you may find you are becoming distracted or even bored. These are just states of mind. Acknowledge them and stay as close as you can to the rhythm of the breath.

The deeper you enter the meditative state, the more you will find that quiet space between thoughts, and the deeper your level of inner peace. As you quieten, it may feel as if the breath is breathing you – a continuous flow of movement. Great joy, equanimity or a profound peace may arise.

When you have finished, take a few moments to bring your attention back to your physical self. Mentally go through each part of your body, naming it silently. Then gently stretch forwards and sideways before you get up.

lifestyle changes

diet Try eating with awareness, as if it were a form of meditation. Eat whatever you want, but before you do, really *experience* your hunger: feel the sharp pangs in your body so that you are aware of why you are eating. Then *watch* your eating. Slowly savour the taste and texture of the food; be aware of your saliva and taste buds responding; be sensitive to the colour, shape and smell of the food, and notice the qualities of the plate, the utensils and the table. Be aware of the food as it enters your body and slowly makes its way through your digestive system – how it makes you feel, and how it nourishes your blood, bones and nerves. As you eat, consider how the food you are taking into your body connects you with the world around you, of the chain of people, animals and elements that is involved in providing you with this nourishment.

Observe those things that draw you away from the simple act of eating, such as the craving to read a paper or a book, of being so engrossed in conversation that you hardly notice the food, or your tendency to swallow without having really tasted anything. What do you learn from such awareness? How can you integrate such awareness into your life?

attitude The Divine is in this present moment, it is the truth of your own free nature. Develop an awareness of here and now, for right now nothing else exists, there is only this moment. Bring yourself back to this present moment whenever you become aware that you are not here and that you have drifted off. When we dwell on the past or dream of the future, we are missing the moment. Breathe into the present moment. Let the 'nowness' of each moment fill your being.

stopping and looking

As Step 7 is about embracing your spirituality, here is an exercise that will help you to see the Divine that is in all things. It will open you to the beauty that there is even in the things that you dislike (including parts of yourself!), and to an appreciation of the magnificence of the natural world.

Every so often throughout your day, stop what you are doing and look around you, and just breathe, just smell, just be aware of this extraordinary place. How did the yolk get inside the egg white, how did the crimson red come into the petals of the rose, how did the butterfly emerge from a caterpillar? How does muddy water find its way up the tree to become sweet fruit? Is there not a magic in this, a grace that moves through all things?

Focus on someone you are having difficulty with and look at the smile on their face, at the sun catching the colours in their hair. See how they may be struggling to be true to themselves, how doubt, confusion or fear are distracting them from their own truth; see that the Divine is in each person equally.

Each time you stop and become aware, notice how your mind has been taking you away into distant places, to other dramas, to the past or to future fantasies – anywhere other than just being here. Let each small encounter with nature – with a leaf, a rain drop or a bird – remind you of the divinity in each thing, each breath, each smile.

the way forward

In completing this programme, you will have reached a deeper understanding of your own level of stress and what you need to do to stay relaxed and efficient. You will also have experienced the difference in yourself. Remember how you were before you started? Take a moment to recall your mood swings or exhaustion, how stress seemed to lurk just beneath the surface, erupting as outbursts of irritation or frustration with little provocation, or making its presence known through headaches or insomnia. See how that compares to how you feel now. Notice how your body and energy levels have changed through doing more exercise, and how your relationships have changed as you have developed a greater sense of yourself. See the effect you have had on others. It can sometimes feel as if you are not getting very far at all – no matter how hard you try, thoughts still fill your mind during meditation and your body totally resists those morning bends. But looking back to see where you have come from shows you that actually you have travelled further than you thought: changes have taken place, you do see things differently, there is a greater sense of balance and ease.

Now your next task emerges – how to maintain your new-found relaxation, and not slip back into old behavioural patterns. You know what stress feels like and how corrosive it can be, so now it is up to you to apply the antidote in the right dosage. You may not want to maintain a full morning and evening programme, but you do need to focus on those practices that you found most beneficial and enjoyable and to create a daily practice time for yourself. A daily practice of just 15 minutes will help you more than doing an hour once a week, since it is the accumulative effect that is most beneficial. Remember that physical movement will release tension before you relax and that you need to be relaxed before you meditate. Use the mini-meditations at any time during the day to bring yourself back to that quiet space. You may also want to repeat this whole programme every few months or once a year to reconnect with your inner self. Or you may want longer periods of relaxation and meditation, in which case you could choose to go on a silent retreat, either by yourself or with others, in an environment that is especially conducive to letting go of stress and discovering ever deeper levels of peace.

To feel alive and to enter into each day with our arms wide, to greet each day with new inspiration, can only happen when we are at ease with ourselves. The practice of relaxation or meditation is not a lazy way out but an opportunity to tune into a vast source of creative energy. It is a means to stay centred in yourself and to connect you constantly to the health, peace and wisdom at the core of your being.

Each one of us is endowed with a great gift. It is our peace. If we are not in contact with this inner well-spring of joy then discontentment will undermine our happiness and create chaos in our lives. When we are at peace then there is one less person in the world who is suffering. We will naturally make others feel better, and we will become more capable, caring and compassionate beings. This is what individually we need, what our family needs, and what the world needs. A relaxed mind is, ultimately, the greatest gift we can give to both ourselves and the world.

Acknowledgements

Most especially we want to thank Leisha Simester for her continual and loving support. Also Pauline Savage for her wonderful attention to detail; and Simon Balley, Vic Paris, Amanda Clarke, and the models Veronica Renshaw and Mike Myerscough, for their unbelievable endurance and good humour in perfecting the photographs. We also want to deeply thank our teachers who so patiently passed on to us their wisdom and compassion, that we might benefit others.

Our gratitude also goes to our families for having supported us in our journey, in particular to Ruth and Ken Leiner and Mort Shapiro for sustaining Eddie throughout his training.

Picture credits

All photographs by Vic Paris except: 13 Photonica/T Sawada; 54 Tony Stone Images/Davies & Starr Inc.; 55 above Tony Stone Images/Davies & Starr Inc.; 55 below Robert Harding Picture Library/Schuster.

The following relaxation and meditation cassettes by the authors are available from:

Eddie and Debbie Shapiro, c/o The Old Church, Monkton Deverill, Warminster, Wiltshire BA12 7EX

SAMADHI – Witness Meditation and Breath Awareness Meditation to stabilize the mind, and develop clarity, self-awareness and innate wisdom.

METTA – Loving Kindness Meditation to dissolve emotional traumas and develop true compassion for both yourself and others; and Forgiveness Meditation to release feelings of revenge, shame or guilt and allow mercy and healing to fill your heart.

KARUNA – Loving Heart Meditation to open to the abiding love that is your true nature; and Heart-centred Inner Conscious Relaxation to release unconscious emotional tension.

SAMATA – Inner Conscious Relaxation to release unconscious levels of stress, clear the mind of deep-rooted fears and tension, and discover a lasting peace and innate joy.

CHIDAKASH – Chakra Meditation to awaken your highest potential through the chakras or energy centres; and Five Element Visualization to free areas of blocked energy and develop higher consciousness.

ANAMYA – Inner Healing Visualization to go within yourself to communicate with your body and gain guidance for healing; and Body-Mind Awareness Relaxation to bring appreciation, healing, love and ease to each part of your body.

index